Gerry Marcotte

Praise for *An Eclectic Gathering*

Gerry Marcotte is a superb writer with an extraordinary gift for expressing his thoughts and feelings…in the form of emotion-packed poetry. In his book *An Eclectic Gathering*, Gerry shares insightful pieces inspired by people and places that have touched his life throughout his journey. I love how he shares his inspiration for writing each poem. Gerry has the ability to touch your heart, stir your spirits, stimulate your intellect and leave you wanting.

—Jamie L. Blahun…Singer/Songwriter…"Slice of Life."

I'm Here
But Not All There

Gerry Marcotte

PublishAmerica
Baltimore

First printing

ISBN: 1-4137-8733-9
PUBLISHED BY PUBLISHAMERICA, LLLP
www.publishamerica.com
Baltimore

Printed in the United States of America

Dedications

To Tim…He continues to show me how important "life" is. His examples, his dedication, his will to become the best he can have been a true inspiration for me. In dedicating this to Tim, I also bring to the forefront Bernie and Merle…a couple of "warriors" living life "One Day at a Time."

To my sons Justin and Andre…In saying "continue writing your stories," this is said knowing that you will at your choosing. Forget not, at some point "change" may be an option. I love you both very much.

Acknowledgments

I'm not sure how to gauge "success." I guess it depends on each individual's perception. My first book, *An Eclectic Gathering*, was a success...for me...because I had few illusions going into this type of market. This success stems from being comfortable with me...and being able to share some of my experiences...my thoughts, my feelings, my ideals and beliefs with others...and being at ease with comments made concerning my writings. This is how I learn and change for the better.

I would like to thank each and every one who has a copy of my book. I received a lot of feedback, which I asked for. A very high percentage favored my style of writing. They felt *An Eclectic Gathering* was "thought induced." Some commented that some of my poems had touched their emotions and feelings. Talk about satisfaction! That's what my type of writing should do if it's to be understood...provoke thoughts, provoke feelings. Therefore, THANK YOU to all who gave comments...As expected, not all were favorable, yet I really do appreciate them. Thank God we're not all the same.

Gerry Marcotte

Gratitude

Once again, to my friend Charlie Goulet, a very big thank you. Like an oasis…his advice, encouragement, critiques, and knowledge have given me a refuge, plus a path to follow…and if I don't stray too far, I won't be left stranded in the desert trying to find my own way.

To my friend Butch B. Because of you I chose this as the title of my book. I certainly identify well with it as I know you do too. Thanks, my friend.

Also to Richard, Vivian, Lillian and Gisele…thank you. Our lives have changed over the past couple of years….and will continue to do so, yet one thing remains constant…our continued love for one another…something I treasure each day.

Gerry Marcotte

Table of Contents

❖I'm Here, But I'm Not All There… 15

❖Dear God, Take Care of Claire. 17

❖Sweet Dreams My Little Child. 21

❖Newsmonger Express. 26

❖A Child's Prayer. 31

❖Mr. Kite, Let Me Fly with You. 37

❖Burning the Midnight Oil. 41

❖Son, My Gift to You 48

❖Thanks, God, for Giving Us Aunty Nini. 51

❖If You Only Knew… 55

❖My Son Jesus's Birth. 59

❖Age, the Dawn of Wisdom. 64

❖Honey Bucket Delight. 69

❖Close Your Eyes…Imagine… 75

❖Help Me to Help You Understand. 80

◆The Pit. 83

◆One More to Kill the Pain. 86

◆Canada's North: A Paradigm of God's Love. 92

◆Life's Merry Go Round. 98

◆Pyramid Poetry. 101

◆Expectations… 104

◆Today…I Never Really Understood… 111

◆Walking the Streets of Individuality. 114

◆And, May You Find Happiness Today. 117

◆The Crossroads of Life (A Tribute to Julie)..... 120

◆A Deadly Seductive Relationship. 124

◆I'm Only a Guest of God's … 129

◆A Young Man's Passions… 132

—It's a Cold Feeling. 134

—A Confused Muse… 137

—Navigation of the Mind. 140

◆My Eyes…The Reflection of My Soul. 143

◆You Give Your Voice So Sweetly. 148

◆Don't Ever Say Goodbye. 151

◆Concerning the Heart, Logic Need Not Apply. 159

◆Love Is Not a One Time Gift. 163

◆Mein Vater. 168

◆Wherever You Go, I'll Be with You. 172

◆It's Neither Here Nor There (but it is)… 177

◆Glossary 179

I'm Here, But I'm Not All There...

If I meditate, contemplate, emulate, advocate,
cerebrate, cogitate, deliberate, ruminate,
concentrate, instigate, debate, interrogate,
rate, slate, exhilarate, curate, desperate...
  Do you think by doing this I'm trying to muse?

Or maybe if I prevaricate, attenuate, probate, grate,
perpetuate, equivocate, debilitate, asseverate,
elucidate, investigate, anticipate, vacillate.
  Can I use these big words as part of a ruse?

What will happens if I demonstrate, celebrate,
create, validate, abate, vaccinate, hesitate,
belate, relate, inflate, irritate, exasperate...
  I guess these are action verbs to use...

Without much trouble, I can bait, date, facilitate,
mate, wait, fate, berate, hate, serrate, decimate,
being late, at the gate, of the consulate, portrait,
act great, be straight, elate, irate, vacate ...
  At some point, folks will assume I'm bemused...

I wonder if I will be constipated?
After all, these words are quite masticated...
I'm really starting to get confused...
The story of my life...what else is news?
I don't enjoy stairs, but sometimes I do stare...
I always try to be fair, yet I hate paying fares...
  I'm Here, But...I'm Not All There...

Dear God, Take Care of Claire.

After hanging up the phone I was shocked...literally shocked. Claire was dead! We had seen her three days prior, and she seemed fine. Now, she was no longer with us...Tears flowed.

Dad was not well, physically, and now he was emotionally crushed. He had no will to decide anything, therefore we, his children, had to decide where to bury Claire. Mom and Dad had bought plots when they had lived in North Battleford. When mom died, this was where she was buried. The decision was made. Claire would be buried beside Mom in Dad's plot.

This poem describes a small measure of the respect I had for Claire. She was such a fine lady. I love her so very much, and I'll miss her dearly. Dear God, take care of Claire. I really shouldn't have to ask, for you will, but being human I want and need reassurances. Please, let me feel her presence once in a while. Is this too much to ask?

If there is to be a reunion, Claire, I guess you'll be the hostess. Until then, give me a poke once in a while, to keep me in line.   I love you.

Claire died June 18, 1986, of a massive heart attack. She was 59 years old.

This poem is based on two Masses: One in Evansburg, the second in North Battleford, and the burial in North Battleford.

Just a note:

Before Dad passed away, he made the decision to be cremated so that his urn would be placed between his two loves. This was an enormous decision for him...He was terrified of the concept, the idea of cremation. Obviously he really did love and respect his two wives, and wanted to be with them in death.

Dear God, Take Care of Claire.

The fragrant, unique smell of incense
quickly dissolved my train of thought.
Claire's casket, an overwhelming presence,
brought on the tears, which I just couldn't stop.
Only questions…What's the answer, God?

Claire never really concerned herself
with what she could get from her marriage.
No…instead she really engaged her wealth…
trying to see what she could bring to it.
And bring she did without any questions.
Love, security and much compassion.

Father's sermon was on a ship in sail,
as it fades into the horizon.
Upon leaving our sight, others hail
her arrival in shouts and songs.
That's dying: To meet The Maker beyond.

Dad had a choice, and made a good one
in choosing Claire. Loved and respected
by all, many a heart she had won
with her winning smile, her honest ways.
Having had a relationship as such,
her memories he'll need as his crutch.

Throughout the service my eyes were not dry,
yet, the sensations I felt in the words
of Gisele's feeling song: "Comme un soleil" *
struck a very emotional chord.
My love towards Claire really soared.

* "Like the Sun."

Claire rarely gave advice unless asked.
She'd listen, perhaps give an opinion,
but usually her thoughts were well masked.
You could use her as counsel or not...your choice.
The ignorant surely wouldn't heed it,
and the wise, well, just didn't need it.

To put Claire to rest...beside Mom's tomb...
was, in fact, a monumental decision.
We didn't want to open old wounds,
for, we still all had a few incisions,
so we dialogued to cause no fission.

Often I felt Claire being smothered
by Dad's overbearing character.
But her passive authority gave her
control, yet, let him feel so important.
When this happened, her sunlight she made,
because Dad could cause a lot of shade.

(At the cemetery)

     I felt Claire was very much alive.
     A real dilemma I faced within me…
     Intellectually nothing seemed to jive,
     so, in my mind I hunted for the right key,
     by letting all my emotions run free.

Claire lived up to her own values,
and worried not what others thought or cared.
Good attitude. She walked in her own shoes.
Claire was quite proud without losing sight of
the powerful strength in being humble.
To remind her, God caused a few stumbles.

     Memories, flooding the conscious mind
     with sorrowful relics of the past.
     The words to say good-bye, I couldn't find,
     so to Mom I sought comfort, plus I asked
     her to care for Claire. Heaven must be vast.

I honestly wanted to say good-bye,
but negative thoughts got in my way.
These feelings, I spent through tear-stained eyes.
I guess this was the price I had to pay.
"Remember, I love you…continue being my friend.
God willing, one day we'll meet again."
Turning, I felt a peace come over me.
"Dear God, take care of Claire. You can, please!"

Sweet Dreams My Little Child.

I've always loved the tune to this verse "Rock a bye baby…" yet, I never put much thought to the words, although I've always felt this wasn't such an appropriate song for a baby. When I came up with the title of this poem, the first thing that came to mind was this verse.

I thought I'd give it a try and see what I felt the words meant…I'm probably out in left field, but this is what I came up with. Actually, the way I understand it, there is certainly a lot of thought, of feelings, of values and ideas expressed in those four lines.

I've written a few poems lately, trying to think like a child or to encompass the child. Up to this point, I had not written much on children before…other than my own, and certainly never on babies.

Talking of babes…Sweet dreams my little child, was a challenging poem because of the context…a baby. They have no past, so to talk merely of the present is a bit ludicrous, therefore I ended up in the future…which may never be attained…merely in dreams.

From this poem all that I ask is that all children have sweet dreams. I know that is an impossibility …but in our own environment we can make this happen…in fact let's make it happen. Kids need love and respect…lots of both.

This poem is dedicated to my precious little granddaughter, Alexis Amelia. With Andre and Nikki's love, chances of successs are certainly there.

Sweet Dreams My Little Child.

"Rock a bye baby in the tree top...
when the wind blows the cradle will rock...
When the bough breaks, the cradle will fall...
and down will come baby, cradle and all."

"Rock a bye Baby in the tree top..."

Your angelic face...so gentle to touch...
your little hands...so soft, wanting to clutch,
but, it's your smile that I love the most...
so innocent, so naive, yet so composed.
I don't believe because you're of my strain
you belong to me. I'm not quite that vain...
No...you're a beautiful gift, merely a loan...
to not only teach, but also to be shown..
that is my obligation, that is my payment due.
I can only hope my style causes few rues.
Why you were sent to me...no clue...I don't know...
but, the pleasure will be mine, watching you grow...

"when the wind blows the cradle will rock..."

Watching you grow, much happiness...and sadness
are already at play...Ah! How I want to caress
your beautiful mind, to protect you from "life"...
but I can't...I can teach you how to survive,
what to look for, how to weather the storms...
Then, it's your choice on how you wish to conform,
how you wish to adhere...after all is said and done.
The winds of change, you'll discover...you'll overcome...
but, if you cause them to blow...well, I can't abet...
even if I wanted to...No! They are yours to fret.
I can harbor your body but not your emotions...
nor your spirit...for they are yours to own.

"When the bough breaks, the cradle will fall..."

Life is so very fragile, so very delicate,
like the bough of this young tree...If you forget
to respect it, causing much strain, much stress...
before long, the branches collapse under duress...
In learning...the same kind of results may occur
on any given day...if you wish not to concur.
Two very important lessons...learn to forgive...
and to love. Don't let these become elusive.
In your life, you will teach me many things...
joy, grief, embarrassment, delight...things I'll cling.
Your Creator has a definite plan for you,
my child. Through people you'll learn the clues...

"And down will come baby, cradle and all."

Everyone, my child, experiences hurt and pain…
everyone…The results asks:"What did I gain?"
That, in essence, is called Life: The Teacher.
The ideas I have in my heart, I want to stir…
I want to instill them into your open mind.
These are my morals, passed on to me in kind.
If you don't attune your thinking with feelings,
when the cradle falls, no doubt you'll need healing…
For the most part, that seems to be the trend…
When this happens, make sure you have a friend,
someone who'll tell you what you need to hear,
who's not afraid to make you look in the mirror.

Sweet dreams, my little child…I love you so much.
I know…my thoughts are in the future, as such…
and I can't go there…We must enjoy this moment,
for, reality…time on this earth…is merely rent.
In your little cradle, you are sleeping so peaceful,
allowing me as guardian…trusting me in my role…
leaving me the key…as "the protector" of your soul.

Newsmonger Express.

A while back I wrote a poem about one of our true heritages...Outhouses, "the laxative of being loose and relaxed."

Now, I feel this poem, our beloved party-line telephones, classifies in the same category...Heritage...and this item should be held in esteem. They were so unique in their look, their sound, and their operation, including crank, mouth piece, and hearing contraption, not to mention the person doing the yakking.

Party-line phones, when introduced, were the main form of communication because it was fast and convenient...for the most part. This was the biggest reason people were connected to this type of system...but, of course, the phone soon became a means of socializing...snooping, and gossiping...and brought much the same results as the outhouse..."the laxative of being loose and relaxed"...only here it was the eardrums and the vocal cord that were put to use.

I, personally, had little to do with this type of communication, for we lived in a "Big" center...this type of phones were for the rural folk. I do recall being at my cousins on the farm, and really having fun...listening to people talk of boring things like the cows, the farm, the chores...but every so often a real tidbit of "important" information was spoken.

Now, a true Newsmonger would not have missed a single word, collected this "useful" data, and made sure no one missed knowing all the "significant" facts...a veritable express line...

Having talked with people who experienced this party-line living on a daily basis, some of the stories were truly funny, some tragic, yet there were some that were very vindictive.

My heritage is of a french background. I wrote this poem using French characters and French expressions with true cultural flavor. It was fun to write...I can just picture these people as described in the stanzas.

It seems every party-line had a "Mme. Aucourant"..."Mrs. Know-it-all"...the ultimate snoop, the true newsmonger, and this person...be it male or female... used the expressway, the party-line, to spread honest to goodness true and pure feces ...and it had nothing to do with bulls!

*** Refer to glossary for translation of French expressions.

Newsmonger Express.

Rrrrr…Rrrrr…Rrr…Rrr.

Allô Suzanne, have you heard the latest news?
Non? Let me tell you! Clemance, that terrible floozy
was talking to Hector, the one who likes his booze…
Anyways, they were yakking about someone's goose,
and the way they were laughing, didn't take many clues
to figure out Hector was the goose who left his shoes
under her bed. Wanna bet they weren't singing the blues?
I can't wait to see them Sunday kneeling in their pews.
I've got to go…Bye! Tonight I'm making a stew…
Oh! Églantine heard she was pregnant. See if it's true.
I'm gonna watch to see if she confesses…such loose
morals. If you have a chance, come and have a few brews.

Rrrrr…Rrr…Rrr.

Allô Marie, Ça Va? Wait till you hear what's goin' on!
Clemance is gonna have a baby before too long,
and the father, that twit Hector Perdant, is long gone…
that's what Alma told me anyways. He tried to con
his way out…what a loser. Good riddance, so long!
Have you heard anymore concerning Yvette Dionne
and her hemorrhoids? Poor girl! What else could go wrong?
Ouch! I hope she bought 3-ply, for when she's on the john.
I'm a bit worried…I have a visit with our calm
Dr. Bonhumeur. He's lucky to have his sweet wife, Yvonne.
I wonder what lyrics 'Grouch Ha-Ha' used in his song
to entice. Whatever the B.S. borne, they get along.

Click…click…click.

Marie? Someone's listening…probably Mme. Aucourrant.
Hey! get off this line. Don't you know your commandments?
"Thou shalt not gossip and be so snoopy during Advent." Click…
Phew! I hope she's gone…man, she can be so belligerent,
so offensive…Her conduct doesn't take much talent.
I heard the Laflammes were out camping, and their tent
caught on fire. Probably Pascal, that slimy ferret,
was the culprit. Oh!..there goes that new elevator agent…
what a hunk! Too bad I'm married…I'd be hell-bent…
I'd better go. I haven't done my breakfast dishes yet.

Rrr…Rrr…Rrr…Rrrr…

Solange! Ça va? What's going on in your life?
Baptisse told me Éphrem wants you to be his wife…
is that true? When will the big day arrive?
In September? How many bridesmaids? Only five?
Curé Le Pécheur needs a collection so he can drive
something other than "Le vieux Bazzou." What can we connive?
You know his sermon 'must be a fisher of men to be wise'?
Make sure to suggest something else…maybe 'sex and arise'…
how it's so important in a relationship to survive.
I'd love to see his face and hear the answer he derives.
The band "Les Désaccords" are very wiry, very alive…
though, often off key…but who cares…they're good to jive.

Rrrr…Rrr…Rrr…Rrr

Allô Marie? I was just talking to Solange Désonier…
Do you know who she's getting married to? 'Ti-Cul le Frappé.'
She is such a ray of sunshine. He's pretty darn lucky!
What's new with Clémance? Is she really seeing 'Le Gros' Ray?
Good match! There's a few loaves missing in his pantry…
and her buns, well, they've shrunk from too much play.
Ramone told me she heard flossy won't be having a baby…
Merci Seigneur! Oh Yah! Pierre, the new agent, is gay…
that's what L'Épouvantail Lise told me…but hey…
I really have my doubts…she always lies straight face.
Ask Mme.Aucourrant…She'll give you the play by play.
Ti-Pit should be home soon. He's usually got lots to say.

Rrr…Rrrr…Rrrr…

Allô, Rosette, how are you feeling? Oh! Lise says "Hi."
When I heard you were so sick, I just wanted to cry.
Is there anything I can do? Maybe cook some tourtières…
anything…I want to help, so tell the truth…don't lie!
Do you hear the clicks? "Hey! There's no need to pry."

Click…click…click…

Maudit Snoops!! So! What's the doctor suggest you try
in your recovery? Nothing? It sounds like something is awry,
something is wrong…Is he telling you you're going to die?
Oh! I'm sorry to hear that. You're so young! My God, Why?
Hearing you talk, it sounds like you're saying good-bye…
Oh chère Rosette, I feel so much empathy…My Oh My!
I'll say a prayer, and offer 'une neuvaine' to the Big Guy.

Rrrr…Rrrr…Rrrr…

Allô Jauklyne, Ça va? Have you heard about Rosette Guy?
Non? Ah! the poor gal is finished…she'll soon be free.
Yah know! I'm thinking about 'Life' and how it should be,
and this isn't the way, not at all…don't you agree?
Here we are being propped on lies of others. We should see
there's more to life than harboring on others adversities…
Right? Yet, la vieille Aucourant spreads it with glee!
Phew! My conscience is informing me of a very big fee,
if I follow her road. Ça m' pue au nez! God! why me?
I mean who's perfect? Who doesn't make mistakes? Gee!!
God knows I'm a sinner, so I'll confess…get on my knees…
Oh! Have you heard? 'Yeux croche' finally got his degree.
I've got to go…Bye.

Rrr…Rrr…Rrr…Rrrr…Rrrr

Allô Fufutt, Ça va? Did you hear about Cecile? Non?…
Well let me tell you…

Rrr…Rrr…Rrr..

Allô Jo-Jo, Ça va? Did you hear the latest? Non?…
Fufutt and Éphrem were seen having a coffee…what next?

A Child's Prayer.

This poem was quite a challenge...for to try and see out of the eyes of a ten year old boy, to use his limited language, yet to try and understand his thought pattern...was intriguing. For a child to try and understand who or what God is, comes directly from the belief of his parents. Now, if the parents are agnostic, in most cases they probably would still give the child some sort of an explanation...so this becomes a God of his parents' understanding...but so what...he trusts that his parents are giving him the correct information, even though his young mind imagines all kinds of different scenarios of what this illusive God is, what He looks like, where He lives, etc.

This child had a problem and didn't know where to turn. His mother offered him a possible solution...at least he was willing to check it out...He had nothing to lose. Here is his prayer.

A Child's Prayer.

"Dear Lord, my mom tells me I need to pray…
Well, I ain't never seen You…what do I say?
Maybe You're too busy, therefore I can delay
this talk…if you want. I can wait another day.
Oh Oh! Mom's getting mad…I'd better not stray."
"Well, I'm not sure how it goes…'Now I lay
me down to sleep'…but I don't…I want to play…
then I can pretend my parents are happy.
I love them and I want them to stay,
yet I'm really scared that Dad's going away."

"Hey! What do You do up there? Play games?
Mom tells me You're a serious dude. What name
do You use? You seem important…lots of fame…
This is the way I understand it. You lay claim
to a famous 'Last Supper', where some guy blamed
You for telling the truth…then he felt shame,
seeing You nailed to that cross, in so much pain.
That musta hurt…That fruitcake was insane…
Mom says they put You in a tomb…to contain
Your body. You fooled them…You left no remains.
    I gotta go…I'll talk to You tomorrow."

"How are Yah today? Are you sure You can hear me?
I don't see how. Is this a magic act that's free?
I gotta say, I slept pretty well actually…
It's been a while, plus I didn't need to pee.
I'm not sure if this is B.S. or just maybe…
You are who You are. Hey! Did You ever want to flee,
to take off someplace where You can just be?
You must get tired of listening to everybody.
Did Yah know that I like sitting in trees?
I often dream I'm flying off to Hawaii."

"My birthday's coming soon. Please, make it fun.
I'd love a bike. Someone stole my last one…
Or, how about a pair of *Nikes* or a set of drums.
What I'd really, really, really like is Mom
and Dad to be happy…call each other 'Hon'.
When they argue, I feel it's something I've done…
I hate it! God, explain to them their son…
that's me…doesn't understand the word gumption.
They say: "Use common sense," yet they have none.
Can You make them quit acting so dumb?"
"Time for bed. Do You mind my talking?"

"I'm in a bit of a funk tonight, even though
it ain't my fault. A friend went and borrowed,
without my consent, Dad's portable stereo…
and wrecked it. My life nearly knew no tomorrow.
Dad's face was so red, it nearly glowed.
I was sure there were going to be blows
…towards me. Dad thought I had showed
this jerk where he kept it. No way…I know!
When I see that creep, I'm going to mow
him with a right if he don't show sorrow."
        "Goodnight Big Guy. Help me with this problem."

"Hey! How Yah bin? Are You still quite near?
Dad says You only drink wine…not beer…
Is that true? Were You popular with Your peers,
turning water into wine? They musta cheered.
When I saw my 'friend', I gave him the gears
for taking that stereo. He has a lot of fear
of Dad…and so do I…He often pulls my ear.
I have a problem…I want You to be very clear.
Mom says this is what You'd want to hear…
that I should forgive that slimy queer.
Whadya think? I think I'll kick his rear."
        "Goodnight! I like talking to You."

"Things are getting pretty bad in our home.
Dad lost his job...now he can't pay the loan.
He's pissed and feels he has a real bone
to pick with his boss, whom he calls 'a gnome.'
I don't know what that is...sounds like a poem
my mom would have read. I wish I was grown...
so I could help Dad...Most everything I own
they bought. Mom blames Dad for having blown
a bunch of money 'on that piece of chrome.'
They need help! Do You think they can be shown?"
        "Think it over, please...I'm really scared."

"Hallelujah! A great job found my pop.
Wow! He was sure down...he needed a prop,
some support, because he was going to pop
someone. I'm surprised he never dropped...
he never slept. Often I'd hear him sob
and mumble...Hey! Was it to You he talked?
'cause he says he's real thankful to 'The Wop.'
If it was You, and I think it was, thanks a lot...
Are You Italian? That's strange...I always thought
You were Jewish...that was what I was taught"
        "No matter, things are better, thanks to You Man."

"Did You know life is getting back like before?
Well it is! Both are happy a whole lot more…
and do you know what? I'm going to the store
and choose a bike for my birthday on the fourth.
If You come, no gift please. You've given Yours…
My parents are together, so I'd be really sore.
I nearly had to pick my mom off the floor
when I told her I talk to You often. She wore
a smile a mile long…she mentioned about a lore…
a parable…When I knocked…You opened Your door.
What's a parable? What door? Man! Questions galore"
       "In three days when I'm eleven…can I still
       talk to You? I hope so. You're my best friend.
       Goodnight, Pal. Do you ever sleep? Love Yah."

Mr. Kite, Let Me Fly with You.

Things are not so hectic at this present time in my life...a sort of reprieve, which is really nice. I consider myself fortunate...fortunate to be able to express my thoughts and my feelings through poetry. This particular poem's debut was fueled by the suicide of a buddy of my son. Each time I hear or witness such a tragic waste of a special human, I feel a real sadness for those who are left behind. LIFE IS A GIFT...Enjoy it to the fullest. For those who find life a chore, there are all types of help. If nothing else, just use your imagination. Perhaps one way is to visualize you are a kite...a simple kite soaring...weaving and wavering in the winds. Just dream of the different types of adventure you could partake...it's limitless...and do you know what? Probably a few of those dreams are more than attainable.

In this poem I've taken a few thoughts, including the consideration of life...on a small journey. On this trip, I decided I wanted to be a passenger...so I could enjoy the ride, and if I had any questions, I could ask...and when have I not any questions? Mr. Kite is my Higher Power, and I do have lots of questions and thoughts...He answers by showing me examples that I could relate to, helping me understand better.

Thank-you, Mr. Kite, for having let me fly with you.

This poem is in memory of Allan Visser, 1981-2004.

Mr. Kite, Let Me Fly with You.

Wow! The winds are strong today...
Do you think I can fly with You?
Why? To perhaps see what's new.
My life needs a good review...
Important things have gone astray.
Priorities change...Who's to say...

Some have told me to "accept the moment
for what it is"...actually to be content...
and to pretend as if it was all meant.
Work with it, not against...Life's too short,
notably if it's one containing good consort...
Gone in a flash. These mem'ries we tend to hoard.

Mr.Kite! Brrr...It feels like rain.
Wow! This dew makes quite a brew...
No matter, this is neat. What a view!
Hey! Do You like the word *misconstrued*,
Mr. Kite? Why am I thinking in this vein?
Anyways, I don't...It causes too much pain.

Some people say they'd love to escape
this world. Not being able to anticipate...
to foresee tomorrow...is symbolic to a rape,
causing them much fear, ravishing their mind.
Well, I say, sometimes I really don't mind
escaping me. A good cleansing is being kind.

Mr. Kite…What happens when You snag?
Does it hurt? Why do I ask? I have thoughts
floating through my brain, which get caught
or lost somewhere, yet appear when sought…
though some…I really have to pull and drag…
Very similar to a game of seek and tag.

My life experiences comes from mistakes…
and really, how many mistakes does it take
to learn? Many! Through them I gain my stake.
Yet, when in those moods, I ask "Why bother?"
And, my answer, "I'm taught all lessons from others."
Some I discard, some I keep, some I consider.

Wow! Mr. Kite! Looking down from this height,
kinda shows me the many ways man can be,
and, in all honesty it ain't great to see…
Man! Are we ever destructible…Wouldn't You agree?
The polluted rivers, all the waste…What a sight.
Of course, no one's responsible…so…no contrite.

Ah Blame! My one time good ole friend.
Time hasn't changed the message you send…
but, in all honesty, I think that depends…
If I put the blame on others for my mess,
then, I should credit them for my success.
Makes sense to me…a lot less stress.

Yet, Mr. Kite, when I look to the heavens,
I can't help but be optimistic…The splendor,
the majesty of the galaxy…all its decor…
It's You, my Creator, showing me there's more
if I continue practicing…again and again,
honesty and integrity…not merely pretend.

Of course, achievements and success are valuable,
but, if happiness is based only on this label…
then my boat is full of holes…disabled…
It's not so much what I do, but who I am
that's important. My desire to be in command
is no longer. Being God is too tough for this man.

Mr. Kite…I know where You're taking me.
Man! I must be a slow learner…I've traveled
this road often…to resolve…to unravel
my ideas, or so it seems. You must marvel
at my thought pattern, giggling with glee,
wondering if I'm finally starting to see.

I need to use my past as a guidebook…
This is my personal study…Therefore I can look
at my yesteryears…to see what it took
to get through…what needed to be discarded,
and why. Using the past today as my card
for the future leaves a lot less scars.

Burning the Midnight Oil.

I was hitchhiking through Northeastern France, in a region called "Les Ardennes." I had left Brussels a few weeks before, had reached a place called Revin, France, and was now heading for Paris. I ended up on a hill just outside of Reims, France, with no luck. That's where I found this really neat refuge. I really remember that time well…actually I stayed at this site for 3 days. It was a very peaceful, quiet, relaxing interlude for me. I really needed it.

I trust too easily…so a few close friends have observed. This poem is exactly about that…trust. Some people don't have a life…They just want to take others' misfortunes and exploit them, making themselves look so good. A bunch of pukes…is all I can say…Get a life!

I was in this predicament when I reached this shelter, and the ole lamp burnt the midnight oil. It turned out to be a cleansing of sorts for me. I remember having made a few resolutions…of which today, I don't remember nor have a clue what they were.

Looking back, I realize I still trust too much…I still get hurt from time to time, and the odd time I'm still burning the midnight oil.

Burning the Midnight Oil.

Standing on a busy highway, thumbing for a ride.
Cars flashing past me, it looks like it's not my day!
I notice up ahead, about a 1/4 mile stride,
a trail leading from the road, that wasn't very wide.
Grabbing my knapsack, I head out along this Way.
Not too far up the path, I find a place to stay.

I am quite surprised, the site's very neat...
well shaded, yet access to a small stream.
I'd be nice, a pickerel or two. That'd be a treat!
Pitching my tent, I start a small fire for heat.
Wow! my sanity is back today, or so it seems.
Maybe not... why do "friends" turn out to be so mean?
Jesus, I hate being used. I could just scream.

Grabbing my rod, towards the water I head.
Not a cloud in the sky, only in my mind.
Casting my line, thoughts appear in my head,
wondering why all those rumors had been said.
I had faith these would stay put. Was I so blind?
I swallowed your facade hook, sinker and line.

No luck, therefore I decide to go for a walk.
This spot is really a hidden jewel...trails
everywhere. I started contemplating on our talks,
realizing I'd been used...what a crock!
During times of my sojourn, I was very frail.
I trusted you with my secrets. Thanks for the betrayal,
Judas!!You had me fooled behind your cape and veil.

My mind's speeding off into outer space.
To slow down a bit, I pull out my flask of rye.
Abusing of my trust, with so little grace,
I want revenge. I want you to acquire the taste
of excrement. You think you're so mighty and high!
Pulling a long swig, I sense my eyes are not dry.

Up ahead, I notice a decrepit log cabin.
I decide to check it out. Wiping the tears
with the back of my hand, I wander in.
In my mind, I wonder what kind of kin
had lived here, how they'd felt, about their fears.
I love the rotting smell, this feeling, this atmosphere.

I note an old hardwood table in the corner.
Wiping off the chair I sit down. I feel so secure.
Images appear in my brain, of issues that were.
Realistically, it wasn't all her fault, for sure.
I really cared for that gal…I thought she was my cure.
Wow! she had the right moves, she knew how to lure.
The skeletons in my closet were taken on a tour.

Dusting off the seat of my pants, I head outside.
I notice a doe and her fawn…cautiously watching me.
This is her home, so by her rules I must abide.
Slowly I move away, making sure to go wide,
not to frighten her. Grabbing my gear, it's time to flee.
That doe and me we's akin…we just think we're free!

Dusk is settling in, so I head back to camp.
Gathering some dry wood, I restart my fire.
The heat feels good, the air is quite damp.
Reflection time…I really wish I could just stamp
that useless, insolent piece of crap. My ire,
my anger asks: "How have I caused so much dire,
so much torment, making you poison the waters?"

Darkness has enveloped me. Looking up to the stars,
I get caught up on how vast the universe is.
It would be so nice to flee, head on up to Mars.
At the rate I'm drinking, I won't be going too far.
I hope my conscience kicks in before I get too pissed.
I know the facts, yet I don't want to admit to this.

Recognition of truth is a humbling experience,
very hard to digest and very tough to accept.
So many lies and half-truths without pretense.
In all my insecurities, I tried to ride the fence,
by blaming others. I needed someone to suspect.
Thinking about it, I gave her so little respect.

The fire, similar to my spirits, was quite low,
so, I added more wood. Sitting back on my stump
I realized I was no angel…I had no halo.
To make me feel good I needed to put on a show.
In the bushes I heard a noise…it made me jump.
In the near distance I could hear a Jack's thump,
relating the news that I was a mumbling grump.

"The difference between stupidity and genius…
is that the genius knew it had limits…you A-hole!"
Where did this thought come from? Need I ask forgiveness?
Wow!! Do I need a drink or what! That's a must!
It suddenly dawned on me…I was searching for my soul,
by looking for the answers in the bottom of a bottle.

In the far distance, I heard the sad moaning sound
of a trains whistle, echoing into the night.
Searching the heavens for some answers, I found
that I fought the current and was almost drowned.
Placing the blame on others seemed so right.
Somehow, somewhere along the way I'd lost sight.

This pursuit of self, this burning the midnight oil,
was taking its toll. The alcohol was in full control.
The booze was drunk; my emotions were in a turmoil,
yet, in my mind there was a different portrayal.
The chaos chose sides: Good against Evil.
I went with my conscience, not with my ego.

The smouldering embers were on their last breath.
Night was fading fast…dawn was inching its way in.
My mind was as hazy as my misty breath.
To continue to live in the past was a sure death,
and to project into the future was a useless thing.
I had to start living today, the best I could, to win.

Packing up my gear, I headed back towards the road.
My mind's weight had shifted. I carried a lesser load.
Sticking out my thumb, my heart felt a wee bit proud…

Son, My Gift to You

You may ask, Justin,"What kind of gift is this?" and you're right! What kind of a gift is this?

My gift, son, is a gift of love, and this gift of love is a small measure of the wisdom that I have gained in my life, and I am willing to pass it on to you...if you want it. Poetry is my choice of transmission.

This poem, Justin, is a brief outline of some of the important issues you will face in your lifetime. May you benefit from the good and the bad and come out ahead.

Always remember, son, you may seek my knowledge. Only you can decide how much you will want or need to be content.

Bonne fête Justin. 18ans...tu n'és plus un enfant. Tu és devenu un homme. Je suis très fière de toi. Je t'aime beaucoup.

Papa.

Son, My Gift to You

May you have much happiness,
contentment, joy and lots of zest.
Enjoy life. Commit a few jests…
But, may you also have sorrow,
at least some. Let a few tears flow.
Be humane. Let some compassion show.

May you have enough success
to overcome personal stress.
Use your knowledge as an access.
Also, may you have enough failures
to keep you humble. It hurts, sure.
Remember it when needs occur.

May you have enough friends
to give you comfort. To commend
you with lots of praise, not pretend.
Also, may you have enough trust
in your own system to be just
and fair. To succeed it's a must.

May you have enough hope
to keep you happy, yet to cope
with problems. Try not to mope.
Remember, keep that smile…
even if you do get riled.
Be strong. Life has many trials.

May you have enough good fortune
to meet your needs, to see the sun
and, while doing it having fun.
May you find a loving God,
just for you, to whom you can talk.
How? Through prayer he may be sought.

I love you, I certainly do…
but you know that, that's not new.
Throughout life you may need a clue…
Come see me, I may have a few
to help you, to get you through.
Son, this is my gift to you.

Thanks, God,
for Giving Us Aunty Nini.

Have you ever taken a personal inventory of your past? Let me warn you if you haven't, it's not that easy. Honesty is the key. I thought I was better or worse in certain situations, and the truth being the opposite. It's an exciting experience, yet quite frightening. Actually every human being should have the privilege of knowing who they are…don't you think?

Writing this poem for Aunty Nini was similar to doing an inventory. Not as in-depth, but much the same outline. Of course I could never be someone else, but in my personal thoughts I tried to imagine some of the experiences Aunty Nini had, for her role in life is as a sister in a religious order, of which she is a fine teacher. Talk of challenges!

This poem is a small outline, a glimpse really, of how I perceived your past 70 years in the religious order, Aunty Nini. I go back to inventory again…Get in tune with who you are, and everything else seems to fall in place. You seem to have done exactly that.

I read somewhere once: "Every man is called to the banquet of life, yet many leave the table starving." As you walk away from this table, I'm sure you'll walk away contented. You'll have shared of a lot of the good things God has left at your disposal. You are such a fine example of love…God's love. We are lucky that you are among us. Hey, God! Thanks for having given us Aunty Nini. We love her tremendously.

Thanks, God, for Giving Us Aunty Nini.

People are lonely because they build walls
instead of bridges. So sad, but oh so true.
Nini may be small, but she sure walks tall.
The language of love is her theme to you.
Always a big smile radiates her face.
So nice to see in this crazy world we live.
She portrays so much wisdom, so much grace.
She demands respect, of which she also gives.

You can give without loving, many do,
but you can never, ever love without giving.
Nini's life, her ways, prove this to be true.
Concern for others portrays her style of living.
She says: "To handle yourself, use your head,
but in handling others, please use your heart."
"Use this simple plan, and you'll be ahead
instead of bickering and being apart."

Many who do as they like are unhappy,
thinking only of oneself. So lonely.
An honest inventory is the key,
instead of seeking only sympathy.
The secret of happy, wholesome living:
To like what you do, not do as you like.
Nini likes helping, caring and sharing.
Being a servant of God feels quite right.

To believe in a Higher Power
and finding out when you die there isn't one,
is easier than when you've reached your hour
not believing and discover there is one.
The Universe is centered on neither
the earth nor the sun. It is centered on God.
Believe not in false prophets or bribes,
for every man's life is a plan of God.

Our whole life is based on attitude,
an emotional feeling, a state of mind.
Lord, Nini has shown a lot of fortitude
in her life. A strong person, yet so kind.
Idealistic yet very pragmatic
so it seems. She has a magic touch.
Also, at times, she seems to be quite mystic.
You know, Lord, we love this gal very much.

About the only thing that comes to us
without much effort on our part, is old age.
It really doesn't matter how much fuss
we create, or if we're illiterate or sage.
Nini has aged well, and so many friends
over the years. All walks of life they come from.
The completeness of life really depends
on what it was lived for, what we've become.

One day we must settle our accounts
with the Almighty. A day of reckoning.
He has the ledger. He knows the amounts.
When the time is right, he'll do the beckoning.
But, until that day, don't stop living,
don't stop loving. Continue making amends.
Live your dreams, your thoughts. See what chance brings.
As a lasting example with no pretends
I say: "Thanks, God, for Aunty Nini." Amen!

If You Only Knew...

I've written similar poems, yet each circumstance is parallel, yet different. Each of us is an individual in specific relationships. The end results of a break-up are quite similar... hurt, pain, anger, fear...but most of us eventually come to grips with this ending...this death of a relationship.

Now, there is the odd case, where one takes matters into their own hands and try to coerce through different tactics. This is usually done by the victim, not the perpetrator.

Well, in this case it's the perpetrator who is threatening the victim...because of jealousy, immaturity...and fear. They realize what a great person they had, so they're willing to use fear as their tactic to get the other back. This individual is sick and needs serious help...but try and tell them that...a little kid's mind in a grown-up body.

A friend inspired me to write this poem...then left. In my life, some people have left lasting impressions...You are one of them...Thank-you!

If You Only Knew...

If you only knew...
the love I felt towards you,
Wow! you'd be so surprised.
If you only knew...
how often I've felt truly blue,
impossible for you to surmise.
> And you'd say, if there's love why sadness?
> Cause love left me open...vulnerable
> to your actions, leaving me incapable
> of halting your pain...inducing much stress.

If you only knew...
that my feelings were always true
towards you...you caused the conflicts.
If you only knew...
that matters of the heart were my cue
to making things work, not logic...
> And you'd say, why is logic so wrong?
> Logic is thought...emotions are feelings,
> and I choose sentiments, for they are healing...
> I opted for the melodies of birds in song.

If you only knew…
how I wished I had wings…I'da flew…
but, my low esteems kept me there.
If you only knew…
the power you possessed…you have no clue.
I gotta say I feared your glare.
And you'd say, who gave you this power?
Well, you took it, with my aid,
then you made me feel like a jade…
a cheater. I never…so why did I cower?

If you only knew…
how often I asked God's crew
to intervene, making things right.
If you only knew…
how often even they misconstrued,
thanks to my lack of insight.
And you'd say, why did I need intervention?
Because anything that was important
to me…values, morals…to you meant
very little. You abused of my sanctions.

If you only knew…
how, at last, my duty to self grew,
to end this one way relationship.
If you only knew…
what my mind wanted me to do…
Not so long ago I'da been whipped.
    And you'd say…my fault we didn't grow,
    but, if I wish to go…there were others.
    I'd be easy to replace by another.
    Well then, cut the strings…let me go.

If you only knew…
how happy I've become…Life continues,
in spite of your renewed provocations.
If you only knew…
how I imagine you in tinted hues…
a fading abstract with much discoloration.
    And you'd say, I was amiss in my thinking,
    and if he harassed me, I deserve it…
    Couldn't I see he was a prize, a hit?
    No! This is good-bye…there's no more linking.

My Son Jesus's Birth.

Most of us have heard the story of Jesus's birth many times. How He was born in a manger in Bethlehem, how He was surrounded by shepherds and their sheep, how they were all guided by this light from heaven...including the three wise men, who in the bible, according to Matthew, were called "Astrologers from Herod's court." They were looking for Jesus to tell Herod, who wanted to kill Jesus. They never returned to Herod, for they felt Jesus was "The King," therefore Herod need not know where Jesus was. Also, a short time after Jesus's birth, Herod was killing all male babies to make sure no new "King" would replace him. Because of this, an angel appeared to Joseph telling him he had to leave and head for Egypt. Like I stated, we have all heard this.

We all know that Joseph was Mary's husband, and the "adopted father" of Jesus, but I've always wondered how Joseph felt throughout all of this...What was his 'take' on this momentous occasion. I can't recall ever hearing a lot about Joseph after the birth of Jesus.

Here is a humble man's version on the birth of his Son.

My Son Jesus's Birth.

"Hey kind sir, could we please get a room?
My wife will be bearing a child soon."
"Sorry! The only place where she may enable,
with warm, dry straw, is in the stable."
"Show us the way…we must get prepared.
Do you know what? I'm a little scared."

"My God! Look at this place, what a mess…
Imagine…to have a baby here…what stress.
Here we are in Bethlehem, this little town,
stuck in a stable, and you're not even down.
Here! Let me clean the sheep and mule dung.
Oh Mary! You're in total grace…and so young."

"What's all the commotion outside. Oh! shepherds.
Their leader said an angel sent them to guard…
He wanted to know what was going on with you,
so I told him…He asked if we were Jews,
in for the census. He said a strange light
guided them. They came in spite of their fright."

"Everyone's hungry…they're all complaining…
so I'll find the market before you start waning.
Is there anything your heart desires, Mary?
No? One of the shepherds will help me carry
the staples. Then, hopefully, all will calm down…
for, very soon…we'll hear the baby's sound."

"I feel the shepherds are very much afraid...
so I'm surprised that most have stayed.
There's mystery in the air, yet it feels good,
therefore, I guess they sense they should
stick around and witness the child's birth...
then be a part of the exuberance, this mirth."

"How are you doing, Mary? Any pains yet?
Do we have enough light? What did I forget?
Gabriel's appearance seems like a dream...
yet, like he said, everything was foreseen.
Wow! You look beautiful, so enthralled...
God knew what He was doing when He called."

"Oh! My darling Mary...a boy...what a gift!
The baby's fine. Your labor was swift.
Listen...The shepherds are bringing their sheep
inside, to bring heat, so our son may sleep.
Jesus is so lucky to have you as his mother...
This night will forever be remembered..."

"Mary! Look to the east...That Star...The Light!
Shining from the heavens. What a sight!
Listen, my darling, time is standing still...
Only the sounds of grazing sheep spills
into this night...Oh! Emmanuel is hungry...
The little Man knows what he wants...so hurry!"

"You must be famished, my love. I'll prepare
leaven bread and fruit for such a rare
occasion. The City of David was favored
for this birth of our son, The Savior...
I sense his life will be extraordinary,
even though He'll try and be very ordinary."

"Look, Mary! The big smile our Son has...
He must be human...He passed a little gas.
Lay down my love, you need a good rest.
I wonder what Abba has in store for our Guest,
for he came from you, Mary, but not of you.
Whatever. We'll love Him dearly, that is true."

"I guess the shepherds have decided to leave.
They've been a few days...since the eve...
and that's long enough. They have much work,
plus, they're to gather more sheep at the fork...
You know the one that heads towards Jericho?
It sounds like their return will be slow."

"Mary! Yahweh has sent three astrologers
from Herod's court. The King wants to lure
us to him. Oh! Look at the beautiful gifts...
Frankincense and Myrrh...The wondrous whiffs
emitted, and gold. They call our son "King"...
To show their respect, gifts they bring."

"Mary, I had a special dream last night…
We must leave soon. An angel in white
appeared to tell me we must flee to Egypt.
It seems that Herod feels he got gypped.
He's searching everywhere for this 'Messiah.'
Let us leave, and become part of the diaspora."

"We are now in Bethlehem, for registration.
I think we'll head for the hills of Judean
and Hebron, then southwest towards Cairo.
Perhaps we could leave early in the morrow…
This will be a hard trip for the two of you,
so, there is much planning I need to do."

"Here, let me help you to get comfortable.
I sure hope this worthless ass is capable
of making Hebron. That dealer seen me coming…
Today he's thanking Allah with a special humming.
How's the little Guy doing? He's sleeping?
Good! Come on you piece of garbage…get creeping…"

Age, the Dawn of Wisdom.

This was a difficult poem to write because I went into territory I'm not familiar with. Why would I choose this type of subject? I find "stuff" like this intriguing, to say the least, and I wondered what I'd come up with, for when I write poetry... in choosing the title, I have a bit of an idea what I want, but when the words start coming, even I'm surprised at the outcome, more times than not.

Even though this poem was difficult, it didn't surprise me, but a few of the verses made me uncover some of my "shoved in the back of my mind" thoughts, to dust them off and examine them anew.

Each of us have our own concept of a Higher Power, for this perception is something deep and personal...If you don't believe, and many say they don't, then just living for the day is the power you are seeking to get through that day.

Religion needs spirituality, but spirituality doesn't need religion. I like that concept...and because I've come to think it through and feel it through, my conscious decision is, today, I do want to go to church by choice, even though I know it can be and is fallible, just like I am fallible.

Is there life after death? I don't know! But in my learnings, in my beliefs, in my limited wisdom, I feel that there has to be something...why would I have a conscience? And if there really is "something," I would presume that it's called eternity, and if that is true, eternity is forever...therefore age is merely the dawn of wisdom, for at this level, wisdom is 'all knowing.' Am I right? Time will tell!

Age, the Dawn of Wisdom.

Age, the dawn of wisdom, what exactly am I seekin'?
To achieve this full development, "Age," I must begin
the process, this happening, "Dawn," and when attained,
then ethics and truth, "Wisdom" will have been gained.

Thinking of "Age," really what does it mean? Maturity?
Becoming mellow? Going the full circle? Being witty?
Actually, it's all the above and much more, withstanding
most of the challenges of life through understanding...
Now our youth! Trying on life with so little planning,
and many are having a very tough time handling
the aftermaths. Why? They lack judgment and knowledge
needed, and desire proper guidance. Like a bridge,
they need to learn to expand their horizons.
Thinking about it, this isn't the dawn of wisdom.

Looking at young adults, the twenty to thirty years,
many act so tough, so strong, yet much fear
is presented through their doings, their actions.
At this age, many are looking just for satisfaction,
because they know everything...they are the fashion,
plus, their physical needs lack a lot of compassion.
This is the age they test their newfound ethics,
only to discard many, reverting to their old mix
received from parents who, actually, weren't so dumb.
I also think this one isn't the dawn of wisdom.

We have now realized middle age, and with it denial,
the disclaimer that we're getting old and the life-style
eventually has to change, even if we don't want to.
By this time in our life we have had lots of clues
provided to us, and several of these have caused some rue,
some regrets, for we never took advantage...in lieu
we became too laid back, and got left behind.
By this stage we navigate slower, but our mind
is still keen. We also realize there's no wand.
The wisdom gained is the darkness before the dawn.

By the time we get to this phase and turn the page,
most people now consider it as part of the 'old age,'
and it's true. For many, our families are so important...
we feel much pride in their creation, much content.
What we've learnt by this time is that when the rent
is due, the rent is due, and this causes significant
change of attitudes...even a bit of humility
for some. The time has come for a check on reality...
Are our thoughts, feelings and actions somewhat correct,
'cause we must 'pay the piper'...he won't let us forget.

But, this period is not all doom and gloom, by no means
for most have certainly not lost the ability to dream,
even though many of their aspirations will not be reached.
Also…this epoch is fertile for those who wish to teach,
as the knowledge to instruct has been instilled in each…
In passing on this 'old stuff' doesn't mean 'to preach,'
because those who most need it will not listen nor stay.
This is also the age where sickness comes to play,
and because of it, a lot experience a need to pray…
yet many are scared, for they've forgotten what to say.

I sense that this "could be" the dawn of wisdom,
for these folks seem to know where they come from.

In trying to imagine what eternity is all about,
it seems when I'm at my ebb I have much doubt,
so I search my soul to eradicate that sore.
During these time I'm cognizant of a closed door…
Upon knocking, the door opens a sliver…not much more,
letting me glimpse…slightly…at what's in store.
I know not why I can't see more…I mustn't be ready…
but for what? I thought infinity was a steady
stream of love and happiness…a total ecstasy.
Did I misunderstand what my teachings portrayed?

But, during my high tide, I desire to celebrate,
to be exuberant, vivacious, wishing to create…
yet, thanking my Higher Power, and to not forget
to ask for His guidance. It's a guaranteed sure bet,
unless I decide to play God…again…then the regrets
surface…again…for I usually end up by owing a debt.
I know if I'm honest and truthful with others and self,
my Creator promises me much spiritual and eternal wealth,
and while on earth, He will sustain me with all I need.
When He wants me, the door'll open, and I will proceed.

Is there wisdom after life? Folklore, I cannot claim
say yes…but many, many feelings I've retained
also say yes! These are intuitions I can't pretend.
In life, when we finally arrive at our day's end,
when our soul departs, searching for The One,
we'll have finally reached the dawn of wisdom.

Honey Bucket Delight.

This is the third in the "Heritage Trilogy." The first written was 'Outhouse Blues,'*** the second 'Newsmonger Express' and now the third…'Honey Bucket Delight.'

All three are 'romantic' subjects from the past…and all three served their purpose very well…in fact some places, the Outhouse is still used. I'm not sure about the honey bucket, and I know that party-line phones no longer exist.

As a young boy, every so often our family would go visit family and friends out in the country. It always was great fun…so much food, laughter, and NOISE. Some farms were starting to get modern conveniences, though some had not. Most places had electricity, but most only had a hand pump for water…or the well, therefore indoor plumbing was nonexistent. In the summer, and winter they used outhouses, yet during the winters, most used the honey bucket…made more sense.

Some of this poem is a figment of my imagination, though most of the things mentioned was taken from different farms and other locations. Actually, on one occasion, while working for 'The Bay Northern Stores,' I ended up in Fort Chipewyan…on a couple of different weekends. Only type of toilet used at that time was the honey bucket. That's another story!

I gotta say to those who never had the privilege of experiencing this type of washroom…you really did miss something…They all stunk, they all were quite primitive, but they all served their purpose well.

As mentioned, some of this poem was a figment of my imagination…thought I wouldn't be surprised if someone told me that this was what their 'Honey Bucket' room felt like.

*** Included in my book of poems, *An Eclectic Gathering.*

Honey Bucket Delight.

We finally made it. Man! Those back country roads
sure are the pits…pushing snow most of the trip.
My complaining didn't help…all I did was goad…
Dad got so mad at my comments, he tore a strip…
I shut-up…His shrouded mind had overflowed
from worry, and I didn't help. I felt like a drip.
Mom baked some cakes and pies for this soiree.
The savoring smells coming off of the trays
beside me were too tempting…I tested…then prayed…

The house was primitive, though it did have lights.
Putting a cover over the food, I pretended to assist…
Lots of people milling around…there was much delight
in seeing old friends…All them ladies wanted a kiss…
Yuck…The ole wood stove, on a cold winters night,
felt so good. I stood beside it…I couldn't resist…
I felt my stomach rumbling…Excitement and nerves?
Ah! I'll try and hold it…maybe…It's getting worse…
Looking for the bathroom, I see the owner. "Monsieur…"

"Hey, where's your can? I really gotta go."
"Downstairs…In the back room…follow your nose…
you can't miss it…the pail that's all yellow,
and the portable seat that's painted dark rose.
Be careful…go down the steps real slow…
The bottom two rungs…well…they're decomposed…
rotten to the core, because of all that moisture.
Guaranteed! Each spring, without fail, this occurs.
I complain, but no action…all we do is confer."

Man! Does it ever stink down here…were's the window?
Will you look at that! A stovepipe for a vent…
Ouch! I'll be!…The seat's cracked…but it don't show.
I guess that's because the darn pail's bent…
on an angle…Do I wonder why? Some of those fellows
weight a ton…That makes sense why there's dents.
I really like the non-existent seat cover…
Wow! What a great help for holding in the odor.
It matters not where you stand…the smell still hovers.

I'd hate to have to be the one that hauls the pail…
Yummy! What a treat! Something to look forward to.
I wonder how many times someone has left a trail?
Where in God's name do they dump this? In the slough?
Imagine this type of ad…How could one fail?
"The Honey Bucket Delight…Instant Perfume…Just For You!
The scent that won't go away! Money Back Guarantee…
Added bonus…The Fish Wrapper Review: "Intimacy…
The Nose that Knows."…All yours for FREE!"

Four reasons that the toilet pail is down here…
as I see it. One: Frozen waste makes less smell.
Two: Doesn't call for a door, which causes some fear,
therefore, you only want to stay a short spell.
Three: No one enjoys a frozen blistered rear…
thanks to the cracked throne. Here, muffles the yell.
Four: Cold is the opposite to money and heat bills…
Now! For those that are looking for a real thrill..
and warmth…long-johns with the trap…without frills.

The toilet paper has the same texture, the same feel
as a brown paper bag...What's the saying:"No pain, no gain!"
Hygiene is not high priority...it's no big deal.
They don't care about some little brown stain
on your fingers...I mean come on, get real...
If so, by the basin there'd be water and a drain.
It's only service now is for cigarette...butts...
Written on an empty bottle of Rye 'Five Star Deluxe'...
"Whiskey gives it, Race Horses do it...The Trots."

Here's a multiple-choice question for all you winners.
"Do you know what you get when you rub pinched
cheeks with rough paper and frozen fingers?"
"A rash? Swearing loudly? Piles? Dirty ginch?"
If you answered "All"...Bulls-eye. You hit the ringer...
Now! To get back up those steps, is no cinch.
Oh Goodie! Look at that...toilet graffiti...
Huh? A Parlor's Prayer! "If the Bucket's what you need...
humility'll take complete care of your conceit."

Heading towards the steps, I pull up my pants.
Taking a little run, I jump and reach the rung.
Someone's tuning their fiddle so folks can dance.
The table's full of food that people'd brung.
A cute neighbor's daughter kept casting me a glance...
I was so shy. Finally I asked her where she was from.
We snuck into a corner...with intentions to observe...
but, I felt she was something I really deserved,
so, I snuck a kiss. Her smile held no reserve...

Party lasted late into the night...Oh! What a fun time.
Finally, we headed for home. The bucket, I never visited
again. For my other needs, the outdoors was just fine,
even though it was pretty cold...I had to wear my mitts...
I wonder how them folks that drank all that 'shine'
feel? Yuck...Tastes terrible, though sure was a big hit.
Them country folk's life-style sure is a deviance...
certainly a bit abnormal...but, great fun...no pretense...
still, I'm so pleased we have modern conveniences.

Close Your Eyes...Imagine...

This poem is really a mish-mash of different thoughts, different feelings, with the idea of letting you use your imagination...by sitting back and visualizing...picturing what you feel or what you imagine it would feel like.

The last verses ask a lot of questions. You don't need to answer them, but if you wish to give it a shot, to try and place yourself in someone else's shoes...a little empathy...you may be surprised by your thoughts, your feelings.

It appears we...all people of the world...seem to have similar types of feelings...and in using this sort of ilk as my logic...then I can say that living in Inuvik or in Bangladesh doesn't really matter. Circumstances certainly are different, but the feelings are similar. Am I wrong in saying this?

Close your eyes...Imagine...You can!

Close Your Eyes...Imagine...

Close your eyes...visualize...
Ah! That smell...homemade cinnamon rolls.
I wonder if mom'll let me lick the bowl...
I'm the oldest, I should have the first go.
Ah heck! Why did my younger siblings have to show?
I start to pout...The nerve! They all laugh at me...
"Grow-up," "Act your age," "Nothings for free,"
Comments that made me madder...They wanted to bug,
and it worked...I punched one right in the mug...
Mom came flying, swinging a big wooden spoon.
Ouch! Sore rear, no rolls, and off to my room.

Close your eyes...let your imagination run...
What's that sound? Man! Am I ever scared...
It's so dark...no moon...My senses are aware...
I heard it again...in those bushes...Is someone behind,
or is it the wind playing games with my mind?
"Hey! If you know what's good for your health,
don't look back...and hurry," I tell myself.
I hear footsteps behind me...I think. I'm petrified!
I sense in the near distance my savior, my guide...
a street lamp. I take off running, turning the corner.
Glancing back, I see nothing...not even that foreigner.

Close your eyes…sit back and pretend…
She told me she loves me…ME…Bring out the wine…
Venus…The goddess of love and beauty is mine.
Very much aware of her own looks, yet so humble,
so unassuming…certainly not searching for trouble.
Waking up, touching…feeling my dream lying beside me…
My perceptions are very keen, very thirsty.
She radiates much warmth, garnering my admiration,
my respect, aspiring there will be no cessation.
I want her so…I need her so…I desire her so…
so…I must reciprocate for our love to grow…

Close your eyes…let your mind focus…
I sensed someone was watching me…I just knew…
Looking around, I was hoping to find some clue,
some indication of whom it might be and why!
Slowly looking through the crowd, I nearly died…
a visage from the past…My ex…I felt a tightness
in my gut. After our divorce, I must confess,
we were not friends. I tried on my game face
and failed…The old reels left a bad taste.
Afraid to restart the projector, I walked away…
To me, It wasn't worth it…I had nothing to say.

Close your eyes...become an observer...
Sundown...To the west, a brilliant orange circle,
slowly fading...entrancing...a magnet's pull,
drawing me to it's cusp. Turning to the east,
dusk envelops me, telling me day has ceased...
Looking skyward, the Dippers and the North Star's
outline hazily discerned by the shapes of the stars,
then connecting the points of light. A full moon
creeps over the horizon. Similar to a saloon...
it sheds blue murky light, creating lots of mystery...
Being one that was drawn, I love the obscurity.

Close your eyes...picture this in your mind...
What color of skin do you think I have?
Black? Brown? White? Yellow? Am I'm suave,
or do you think I'm a con? What sex am I?
What's my age? If hurt or sorrow, would I cry?
What country would I call home? Is there war
or peace? Do I walk, ride a camel or drive a car?
    To be honest, trying to portray someone other
    than myself is difficult...To become a daughter
    or a mother, or to represent a different color...
    To envisage my existence with little or no water,
    or to live my whole life in fear and terror...
    Merely thinking about it makes me shudder.

Close your eyes...imagine...
My dwelling...Are there many in a small room,
or few in many big rooms? Is there wealth to groom
my education or am I illiterate...perhaps a beggar?
My beliefs...Allah, Budda, J.C. or something better?
Am I Liberal, Socialist, Communist or some fake?
Do I believe in love or am I programmed to hate?
To imagine myself having so much control and power,
subjecting people, on a whim, to beg and cower...
no thanks...I imagine myself climbing that tower,
to destroy 'The Clock of Doom' before the appointed hour,
giving back to the people their rights, their power...
Imagine...No need for graves...No need for flowers.

Help Me to Help You Understand.

My friend Jamie Marks-Blahun asked me a long time ago to write some verses and see if she may be able to put music to them. I didn't feel comfortable at that time, so I put it off. Not long ago I decided to give it a try, but not so much as words to a song, but as writing a poem with a bridge included.

This poem is really a generic sample…situations like this have happened to so many women…and men. It's a poem looking at one of life's greatest joys, or one of life's indescribable pains…LOVE. Everyone can identify with this…right?

Poems have been written on every type of emotion or feeling. It's nothing new. The only newness is my slant or version…and that, really, isn't even so new … but, just the way I put the lines together may give someone a new outlook.

Will music ever come to this poem? I really don't know, nor does it really matter. As for Jamie, well she's now into different types of music, plus, she has a gift for creating a tune of which she puts her own words to. She writes very well without me.

Help Me to Help You Understand.

I see sadness in your expression,
and the misty tears in your eyes.
I see the way you look around,
hoping no one's seen you cry.
Finally, you've unveiled his disguise…
A user, pervading you full of lies.

Again, he's hurt you, babe, just like before.
You keep going back to him, still wanting more.
You're in denial, girl, and don't even see it.
You encourage him to continue inducing conflict.
If you persist on his approval, why should he quit…
and gal, that is so wrong. Come, hold my hand…
talk to me…help me to help you understand.

You're such a kind, giving person,
good looking and quite smart…
I know you know, deep in your heart,
that this can't keep going on…
Despite the fears of a new start,
you'll soon be willing to part.

Whispers and gossip around town,
are telling me he's been using you...
It seems he's found someone new.
Let the tears flow, say good-bye...
you honestly deserve someone true,
to make you smile...not feel blue.

Come, I want you to take my hand...
help me help you understand...
to show you that time is like sand...
slowly sifting through your hands.
Time'll show...you deserve a better man.

The Pit.

I have just written a letter to my friend Dale, a few hours ago. Writing to him made me think of the shack we shared and called home while living in Cold Lake, Alta. We both worked in the meat shop at the IGA in Grande-Center, which is now Cold Lake.

During this period, I owned a convertible, was dating Rachel, made sure there was lots of action, and we lived in a house that became known as "The Pit." Dale helped make most of this possible. He was a great guy to live with. We have some great memories other than this house, but we also have some great memories of "The Pit," our pad. Oh Yah! The interior decorating was something else.

The Pit.

A very small shack with four rooms,
the kitchen sink with the bath.
A fish net hung on the wall.
"Welcome" the motto of our pad.

There were pinups on the wall,
and pictures everywhere above.
Many a person came single,
also, many with their loves.

"Help us out: Bring your own booze,"
was what we asked…a password.
When everyone would abide,
it was enough to scare the Lord.

Anyone that entered our pad
had to sign our famous bust.
Many a name was written,
for this was an absolute must.

Many a person who came here,
always seemed to be on the make.
They were much like our curtains...
all different sizes and shapes.

Though fluorescence was our colors,
black seem to be our only light.
Music, the speakers were screaming,
we lived only to revel at night.

Labeled as "The House of Sin,"
we had a bad reputation.
A lot of parents thought:
"For sure, they are the Satan."

Our furniture was scarce,
but this joint was a big hit.
Man, just about everyone came
to our shack called: "The Pit."

One More to Kill the Pain.

It's been a while since I wrote about my illness. Every once in a while I need to do this, to remind me of where I came from, what my thinking was then, how I wanted no commitments, no responsibilities and how easy it was to blame others. Wow! I have changed...for the better.

This poem brings back a lot of memories. I was never married when I was drinking, yet, everything I talk about in this poem I've felt in the different relationships I was involved in. I always wanted to take, but I wasn't too willing to give...which ended up being my downfall with most of the women.

Alcohol was my best friend, therefore I couldn't surmise that this was my problem...I mean, usually a best friend helps you, not destroys you. Therefore, when I was in turmoil, or had my doubts, or needed someone to understand me, I went to my best friend... alcohol. He always stuck up for me, and led me to believe that I was right and these others were wrong. Often, with this type of reasoning I was always taking one more to kill the pain.

Thank God I have faced my demons and come out ahead. If I need to kill the pain today, I will use communication, I will use my support system, I will use my Higher Power, I will use whatever positive means at my disposal. Being an alcoholic, I have to be very much aware of the choices I make, for anger, fear, resentment...to name a few...could cause my former friend back into my life. No Thanks!

One More to Kill the Pain.

Alcohol, you beautiful, fermented friend,
always there to help sooth and defend.
Through my actions, my story has many blends...
Of course, I do little wrong, so few amends
are needed. I sure in hell won't take the blame.
Ah! Why not...One more to kill the pain.

Halfway down the street my nose sensed it,
so I hurried to get there as quick as I could.
Swinging the doors, I searched for a corner to sit.
Ah! A double shot of rye would taste good...
to settle my nerves. Phew! It'd be nice to forget,
but that won't happen. I curse the day we met.

I need to contemplate, mull things over a bit...
figure out all my options, all the things I should
or can do. Finally! my drink's coming...Ah shit!
I left my smokes at the shrink, Dr. Woods.
Man! That guy's a real quack... asking all
those stupid questions. He has a lot of gall.
    Thinking about questions and answers...

How come I figure out all the answers sitting here?
Man! Am I smart! Yet, as soon as I tell her
my thoughts, the fight starts…She don't want to hear.
I wish, at some point, we would be able to concur,
instead of me always yelling, causing her tears…
I feel like a heel each time this occurs.
I have volumes of buried thoughts, which I fear
will be left where they are…No sense to confer.

Hell! I'm having one bitch of a day, actually
I'm asking myself, what to do? what's the right way?
We've been feuding for so long, we hardly agree…
My ole lady will argue today is not really today.
Why do I like the feeling of this here place
way more than home? Because I can enjoy my space.
  Oh Oh! Now what's my mind thinking….

Tell me, what does the word humility mean?
Is it similar to humiliation? Sounds the same!
The dictionary says '…be humble', not to be mean…
but, that's hard for someone who is extremely vain.
You like putting me down quite often…so it seems…
to better yourself. What do you want a little fame?
In your own eyes, you may think you're a queen…
but, in the eyes of others you ain't no dame.

"Hey! Bring me another double, I'm thirsty...
and, while you're at it, a pack of DuMaurier."
The bar gal glared. "Darlin'! If you need to pee,
use the toilet out back, you don't need to pay."
Women! Jees, you'd think I committed a crime!
Another dirty look, and I won't leave a dime.
  Now, where was I? Oh yah!

  Memories...like an alluring drug you can ride,
  stopping to change the image with words that soothe.
  In my recalls, I visualize quite often you lied...
  or did I just surmise that you had taken the fruit?
  I, also remember when you felt so much pride...
  or, were you showing off on how to become a prude?
  I hate memories, I really do. They become modified
  or capacious. No happy medium, merely half truths.

Wow! I feel good...I'm starting to get a buzz.
Look-it there! A pretty gal ripe for the taking...
Nah! Better not...all the problems it'd cause.
Been there, done that...and took a real raking.
Ah! What's the difference! I'm already in trouble...
"Hey pretty lady...let's you and me share a double."
"No? A boyfriend?" A well...What was I was thinking...

Now, resentment…that there's my type of word…
The old bag treats me like dirt, then wonders
why I get so mad and feel so bitter towards
her. We're opposites…like fire and thunder.
She loves wounding me with her words…her sword…
slashing her disdain. I want us to be asunder.
Why can't she see? Please help me dear Lord…
Talk to her, make her see my way…not to blunder.

Alcohol, you beautiful, fermented friend,
always there to help soothe and defend.
Through my actions, my story has many blends…
Of course, I do little wrong, so few amends
are needed. I sure in hell won't take the blame.
Ah! Why not…One more to kill the pain.

My head's spinning, I gotta go for a leak…
"Darlin', bring me a 'Tequila Sunrise' with lime.
I'm goin' to the can…doan' make it too weak."
Wooh! Quit lurching. What's the time? Only nine?
Missed supper again! Ah well! What's the big deal?
No doubt get my usual…The Cold Shoulder Meal.
Don't need that, I'm stayin'. Where was I…

She's always complaining about my drinking.
Excuses, excuses! So I likes to drink a bit...
I hardly get into trouble...It's all in her thinking.
What does she want me to do? Sit at home and knit?
Yah! Right! She makes such an issue about me winking
at some blond or brunette...and has a real fit.
I mean, they were good looking...So why this inkling,
this suspicion, making me feel like a piece of shit?

I guess I'd better go. What's my excuse tonight?
I know...Tex, from work, needed someone to talk to.
Indeed, he did offer to buy. It took all my might
to say no...He's clueless...His brain has nothing new.
I shouldn't pick on the poor guy...not his fault...
He's always getting hassled for tasting the malt.
Here's to you Tex...One more to kill the pain.

Walking outside I meet my lost friend, Mr. Sun...
He's heading for home too. I wave goodnight.
This playing games with my mind is no fun.
I need a drink to help me gain some insight...
Oh! I can already feel the furnace's blast.
At this rate, we just ain't gonna last.
Ah well...C'est la vie.'

Canada's North: A Paradigm of God's Love.

When I left home many years ago, I stared working for 'The Bay, Northern Store.' After a short stint in Fort Nelson, BC I was transferred to Fort Smith NT.(Back then it was NWT). Fort Smith was an excellent teacher for a young guy like me... everything I wanted and desired was there.

Fort Smith is located on the eastern border of The Wood Buffalo National Park, yet to get to it by road, for there is only one road, you have to travel many miles in the park. While living in Ft. Smith, I traveled that road many times, always enjoying the beauty. Most times there seem to be buffalo crossing the road, or near the road...grazing and minding their own business...or wolves. Even the odd bear.

The thing I loved the most about this park was its bigness with very few people disturbing the nature. It really is an outdoorsman's paradise...hunting, fishing, skiing, canoeing, or hiking the many trails, plus, of course, the traplines, dogteams and sleds. I'm not that much of an outdoorsman, yet I loved the peace and quiet, the vastness of my surroundings, the feelings of oneness.

This poem is about nature. These similar experiences have happened in many different places by many different people, yet no one can have these same feelings...because they are mine. I've experienced many paradigms of God's love...in His showing me the beauty in nature that He provided...the Rocky mountains, the setting sun, the distinction and fear of an electrical storm, and much more, yet The Wood Buffalo National Park experiences stand out as truly one of a kind....for me.

Just a note. The people of Fort Smith, during this period, were a refreshing, friendly bunch. I made a lot of friends while living there, and had a great time doing it. Many thanks.

91

Canada's North: A Paradigm of God's Love.

Canada's north is so vast, yet, so much character...
The McKenzie River, Two Great Lakes, the Nahanni Falls,
the Alaska Highway, Rocky Mountain Range, and much more
My most memorable emotions were experienced
in and around The Wood Buffalo National Park...
I love the bountiful streams, rivers, and lakes...
The Land of the Midnight Sun...and total darkness...
The contradictions I savored of summer and winter.
The north is so big, with a beauty that can best
be described by truly tasting its remoteness...
by listening to it's beautiful silence...yet to feel
an awareness of the life and the sound all around...
For me, it was a dream fulfilled...I love the North!!

Driving through the Wood Buffalo National Park
late one night, the tires of my truck
crunching a tune on the snow crusted highway,
I sensed lights to my back. Looking in the mirror,
the expansible heavens had become a dance floor.
This night the Northern Lights were the entertainers...
the Aurora Borealis...and did they put on a show!
They were jumping and dancing in all directions.
Very soon I was totally engulfed by their maneuver.
Pulling over, I got out of my vehicle and watched...
In describing this ritual, this wonderment of movement,
is knowing that man could never imitate this feat.

I observed this phenomenon, this wonderful magic...
wavering and weaving...using the stars as their background.
Being conscious of my surroundings, I felt encompassed
by a music...a creaking, popping sound in the air,
in tune with the harmonizing timbre of wolves howling.
Looking at the lights I notice all these colors...
some greens and reds and blues, and of course silver...
various intertwined, clinging and moving all over the sky,
following to the beat of this vibration, like a tribal dance
while others wanting to be alone, did their own thing,
followed their own patterns, moved to their own beat.
My mind's telling me this is God's show, His spectacle.

This was my first time for both...dog sled and trapping...
a gift from Ole' Gus for supplying him with dog bones.
"What the hell are we doing out here?" I thought to myself,
"I mean it's only twenty below, with a wind chill
of thirty below zero. Total, absolute asinine!"
Even though I was cold on the outside, I was warm inside...
and why not! This was something I'd only dreamed about,
never expecting this to become a reality...Never!
We'd left Ft. Smith, followed the Slave River south
to Fitzgerald and on to Hay Camp. It was total darkness,
except for a hazy mid-morning light. Though I was whining,
I felt a sense of freedom I'd never relished before...

Gus checked one of his traplines…nothing! I was caught
in a paradox…I was sad he snared nothing, yet glad…
I didn't want to see a marten or a fox mangled
by the traps, yet ole Gus needed food for his table,
by way of the skins he acquired. This was his livelihood.
His lead dog was part Siberian Husky, part Wolf…
and when addressing his team, he spoke harsh in Chippewan,
usually to his lead dog, who settled the rest quickly.
Moving on, we arrived at this log/mud trapper's cabin.
Gus wasn't much of a talker, yet I felt quite accepted
in his solitude. On this cold, clear arctic winter's night,
bundled warm…I felt at peace with nature and man.

I bought a Honda motorbike, thanks to my friend Stan,
who had bought one also. The staff house we called 'home'
was never the same…bouncing off the walls with our bikes…
Finally, The Bay transferred me to Hay River's New Town.
I love traveling through Wood Buffalo National Park…
it really is something to behold…remote pristine forests.
My bike and I saw only one truck in two hours.
I stopped to eat by a river. Hearing sounds behind me,
I saw this herd of buffalo…these big, shaggy heads
watching me with curiosity. Sensing no danger or threat,
they crossed the highway and headed into the forest.
In the stillness and quiet, I watch them disappear.

Suddenly, I heard this ruckus…looking around again,
I see this crippled large framed bull buffalo with
the short blunt horns, trying to keep up with the herd,
but he can't. In the near distance I sense, then see
a few wolves. The fear shown through his dilated,
frightened eyes and his jerky, uncoordinated movement,
tells me he's keen to the smell of these predators,
and knows they are near. When he noticed me, he became
quite confused, sensing more danger…not sure which route
to take. I made no movement, for no doubt he felt trapped.
Limping across the road into the trees, this poor animal
had no chance… survival of the fittest dictated this.

Getting up to leave, this feeling of being totally alone
engulfed me. I felt the power of nature surrounding me…
an intuition stating: This was a paradigm of God's love.
I sensed a peace come over me never experienced before.
I felt I was the only person in the universe…so free,
not a care in the world. Unwittingly I became an observer…
detached, looking in a mirror, seeing the road ahead,
and in the reflection not quite sure what to make of it.
Slowly, I got up, kick-started my bike and drove off…
leaving this sketch behind, for practicality set in.
My mind went back to that wounded animal, wishing,
yet, realizing with regret that I couldn't help.

Over the years, I've returned to these parts
merely a half dozen times, yet the feelings
are still the same, they haven't changed at all.
For me, it's similar to that first drink...
a physical, mental, and emotional change occurs...
no control of knowing when the end will befall,
and hoping it won't. The power felt is intoxicating...
exhilarating, empowering...giving me authority
to try and re-experience those same sentiments...
to relive those moments and rejoice in their memory.
This paradigm, one example of God's love for me is...
The Wood Buffalo National Park. My love for God
is in accepting this treasure and saying thanks...

Life's Merry Go Round.

John, a friend that I shared a house with in Drumheller Alberta, asked me to write up a few verses...He had this tune that needed words. Also, he had an idea of the type of song he wanted, so he wrote part of the first verse, then asked me to finish it for him.

John is a very good twelve-string guitar player, plus an excellent singer. About the time I got to know him, he had bought himself an electronic drum system to accompany him when he performed his gigs. He really was/is the quintessential one-man band.

It was fun writing this piece. Not to complicated. I left Drumheller not long after this, and unfortunately I lost contact with John, so I'm not sure what ever became of this "song." Whatever...here are the words. Don't judge too harshly.

Life's Merry Go Round.

Tell me what you are doing
when you stay out late at night.
You say you weren't a cheatin',
but your hair sure looks a fright...
You say the wind was blowin',
that you only had one beer.
Then tell me how did the lipstick
get from the neck to the tip of your ear.

It seems always the same old story.
Ask a question...answered by lies...
then, accusing me of no trust...
through it all pretending to cry.
I try to cure this bad disease
by moving about, changing towns.
The only changes are her men,
on the roller coaster ride she's found.
Welcome to: "Life's Merry Go Round."

You really must be quite an attraction
at all the "meetings" you seem to attend...
for every tomcat around is on the prowl,
fighting over that scent that you send.
You say I'm just making up stories,
and anyways, the guys are all queers...
Then tell me, how did the lipstick
get from the neck to the tip of your ear.

You always leave me at home…
I still never figured out why.
Your friends are very, very good
at mooching and straight face lies.
You keep say that I don't listen,
but, you just don't want to hear…
when I ask you how the lipstick
got from the neck to the tip of your ear.

You say you love me the very most,
I mean…I should know by your feelings.
I seem to ask myself if that,
with time, there'll come a healing.
You say that your friends are true…
just by their reflection in your mirror.
Then tell me, how did the lipstick
get from the neck to the tip of your ear.

Pyramid Poetry.

When my book "An Eclectic Gathering" came out, a young fellow by the name of Jay Stewart recognized me from the picture on the back of the book...a copy his grandmother had bought. I had the pleasure of having supper with him and his grand-Mother, Marie. In conversation, he asked me if I'd ever written "Pyramid Style Poems." I said I hadn't, but some day I might...and I have. Thanks Jay.

This was fun writing...not too complicated, but certainly a bit disjointed. I wasn't sure the outcome, though I rarely do on any of my poems.

Looking over the poem, actually it's quite neat the way it progresses. In the first verse, the guy's in denial, though he knows, by the way he speaks, he may have a small problem with booze. By the second verse he's admitting to being a bit lazy, tries real hard to evade work...with the help of like-wise buddies. In the third verse, he's saying that he hangs around bars, but he sees how it's affecting some of his buddies...not him, of course. And the fourth verse, he mentions his good buddy Joe, who may have a small problem with booze, but more so "stress." He can't acknowledge Joe's behaviors, for they're in tune with his...therefore back to blaming others. He went the full circle.

Make what you want of the poem and this type of writing, but I gotta say, it's something I enjoyed trying. Thank-you Jay.

Pyramid Poetry.

I
can fly
my kite high,
even enjoy a rye,
if I desire to deny
my booze problem, as I try
to account for this, using the guy
next door as my reason to simply lie,
to self and others, as I pretend to cry,
thinking that I am so smart, so very sly.
Folks shake their head in repel and sigh,
asking when had I started to comply?
Unsure. Maybe because I was fried?
No doubt. I'd better supply
this with a reply,
just to verify,
I buy
my
ice
at sunrise,
cold, no surprise.
If some prying eyes
wished to lurk and surmise,
like the third of my ex-wives
use to do, thinking she was wise,
talking behind my back, spreading all those lies,
telling everyone I never worked, drank and ate fries.
What a stinking liar! I ate chop-suey and rice.
I hate fries! The rest I won't justify...
I worked! Sometimes me and the guys,
we'd sit and try to contrive
a thorough plan to disguise
our need to strive.
After many tries,
our devises
subsides.

So
we know
where to go...
Some place to burrow
all our feelings of woe.
Big deal! We had to undergo
therapy. Why do folks want to pigeonhole?
Our tavern buddies...man...they like to borrow
each other's truths...and those truths, sure do grow,
especially when the good spirits really start to flow...
Some of them, their red nose's amazingly glow...
like Rudolph's does at some reindeer show.
These guys drink too much Ouzo...
For example, take Old Joe...
He lives today thorough.
For him tomorrow
merely shows
sorrow,
pain,
no gain.
Life's a drain,
so tells his brain...
in segments,frame by frame.
Other times he feels like pray'n',
but, he forgets what he was say'n'.
His friends think he's suffering too much strain,
certainly not drink...though at times he should refrain.
One thing he needs to learn how to contain
is his anger. Wow! he goes right insane,
but really, who am I to complain?
Many times I'm not too sane...
yet, as friends we'll remain.
We understand the game...
There's no shame...
puke, stain,
blame...

Expectations...

There is an expectation to every action we do in life...If we buy something, we expect it to function for a certain time ...especially if we paid a lot for this item. When we do a good deed, we expect, at least, a thank-you. When we do bad we expect to suffer the consequences. For every action, there is a reaction.

Now, why did I write a poem on this topic? I am more of a reactionary type person than one who responds...to problems, to circumstances, to issues...therefore my expectations, at times, seem out of wack...they are usually too high...but then, I often put high expectations on myself.

Over the years I have found more of a balance in my expectations...therefore I'm not so surprised, sad, overwhelmed, happy, mad, disappointed...and the list goes on...which is certainly better for my stress level. Sometimes, though, I get a rude awakening. Then, my imagination takes me on a journey that, at times, is scary. That's when I have to get in touch with reality, and to look at this incident at face value, then make a sane decision. Today I am capable of doing so...A little growth?

I only chose four topics...parent/child, child/parent, spouses/concubinage, friends. I could have chosen many others, but in these four, I covered a lot of emotions and feelings...the main reason for expectations. These four topics I chose have had the most joys and disappointments...and still do today. There were others, like siblings, jobs/vacations, etc, that were also important, but I had to draw the line somewhere.

By examining this 'state of mind', for I feel that's what expectations mean to me, it has helped me understand a bit more what to expect from life...to try and keep it on a low key...not desiring too much or too little.

Will writing a poem on this topic help me change? Probably not...Mais, que veut-tu?

Expectations...

As a kid there are certain rules to follow...
Do your chores, not cause too much grief,
and to have respect. Now, there's a feeling...
actually, a bursting soft spot near my heart,
which has my child's name on it. Sometimes
this spot is called pride, sometimes rejection...
and many emotions in between. What's the cause?
Expectations! I want them to follow my agenda,
yet, it's their life! What a paradox I've created.

Parent/Children:

He's going to be a 'superstar'...look at him go...
He'll need lots of dedication and hard work,
but who cares...Man! My pride is exploding...
everything I ever wanted, he has the chance to be.
    "Hey Dad! I've decided I'm not playing anymore...
    It's no fun...the coach is asking too much of me,
    and honestly, I don't see this as my future...
    I just want to hang out with my friends...Sorry."

I wonder what University he'll want to go to...
His marks are very good. He must be a brain,
for he never studies and he's doing so fine.
I can hardly wait for him to be valedictorian.
    "Dad, the principle wants to see us both...
    I think someone squealed on me for cheating.
    I don't know what the big deal is...So what?
    It's not like I'm the first...Lots are doing it."

Wow! My child has achieved so much more than me...
Look at all his toys...He's making big bucks...
I guess...Money seems no object. I'm so proud.
Material wealth appears to make him important.
  "I hate asking you, Dad, but I need some money...
  I got laid off...My job is classified 'redundant.'
  How could this happen? Phew! Ego deflation time...
  Oh! Can I borrow the car? Mine got repossessed."

            As a parent there are certain rules you follow...
            Food, shelter, clothes are but basics...Everything
            else is a bonus...love, respect, communication...
            Parents, often, are such hypocrites...They say
            one thing, yet do the opposite..and then expect
            us to follow in their footsteps...be our role-models.
            No thanks! We kids bargain on so much more in life...
            A dream? Not sure! We're searching for consistency.

Child/Parent:

Why do my parents always tell lies? They promise
me the moon when their drinking, giving me false hope...
but when sober...they're all apologies and excuses.
That really hurts! Who can I trust if not them?
  We feel so bad, promising all those goodies,
  but, we just don't have enough money. Booze's expensive.
  We should shut our trap when we start our drinking...
  It always gets us into all sorts of trouble.

Dad said he was gonna make it to the concert...
So where is he? This year is no different...
I guess I'm really not that important to him.
I love him so much...Why does he always lie to me?
What a dilemma! If I don't promise her to come,
she's disappointed...yet, because of my type of work,
I never seem able to make-it...and I feel terrible...
She's tired of her expectations being crushed.

My Dad always embarrasses me with his mannerism,
especially in front of my friends...Ooh! I hate it!
Why doesn't he act like a responsible adult...
instead of his phony "hip?" He thinks he's so "cool."
My kid complains I don't interact with his friends,
so, when I try and partake in their discussion,
he makes quite a scene. Which "F" does he really want?
"Father," "Friend," or "Foe?" I'm totally confused!

Expectations hurt...unfortunately...
Frequently, too much emphasis is placed
on my anticipations. More often than not
my goals, my targets are too high, so it seems,
especially when dealing with spousal matters...
In all actuality I should have supposed
very little...yet, I want so much for us.
Expectations hurt...unfortunately...

Spouses/Concubinage:

Sex! It's always been a contentious issue…
We rarely agree. For me, the moods and feelings
are so important…this is a gift…a gift of love…
shared together, conveying intimacy for each other.
　　　What's so complicated about wanting to make love?
　　　Even religion states…to have a happy relationship,
　　　partners must abide by the conjugal rights…
　　　I love my wife a lot…so, I expect my remedy.

You know! It's all those little things…raising the seat,
not picking up, making excuses for being late…
and the list goes on…Then he wonders why I'm mad.
Be respectful and help…plus a little courtesy…
　　　Why is she complaining? I mow the lawn, shovel snow…
　　　I know, I know…She takes care of the kids,
　　　the cooking, the cleaning, the garden…and a lot more…
　　　I'm grateful. Perhaps though, she expects more from me?

It's a given…there's another woman involved…
She's called "La Job," and she doesn't like to share.
Spending quality time together is expecting too much.
I feel acrimony…His job seems more important!
　　　What seems to be the problem? If we want the toys,
　　　it takes cash…therefore I put in the extra time.
　　　We want the boat, cottage, skidoo, holiday trailer…
　　　All our friends have them…So, what do you expect?

Now friends, you pick and choose...unlike family,
where you have no choice...you get what you get.
This friend, if a true friend, will tell
you what you need to hear...not necessarily
what you want to hear...and anticipate the same...
You will expect trust, loyalty, confidentiality.
But...if this "friend," through manipulation,
leads you astray, be aware of your anger and rage.

Friend:

"Hey buddy, I'd appreciate if you could loan me
some cash. Everything's happening in bunches...
You know what I mean? I'll pay you back real quick.
I'll have you caught-up in a couple of weeks."
        Funny! I haven't seen or heard from Sam in a while.
        I wonder if he's sick? Sure wish he'd pay me back.
        I have a feeling it's because he owes me money...
        Man! That hurts...I thought he was a good friend.

"I hear that you're having tough times. Can I help?
You know I won't tell anyone. Sometimes you need
a shoulder to lean on. Trouble on the home front?
You and the wife spatting? I know, I know...It's rough..."
        What's going on? Everybody knows what's happening
        in my marriage...and the wife is furious...Oooh!
        I needed to talk, so I trusted this "true" friend.
        Thanks for violating my confidentiality.

"Hey! I heard some rumors about your past...
Wow! It sounds like you were quite the guy...no angel...
This person spreading the manure is an ole buddy,
or so he claims...What kinda friend is that?"
What a life! The past'll slaps you in the face
every time, especially when a ghost appears
from that era. Those that wallow in this filth
are not friends, yet their vindictiveness hurts.

Expectations are truly a state of mind...
They are so demanding...asking so much from me.
It affects my joy, my happiness...all emotions...
especially if what I expected doesn't come true...
then my sorrow, my disappointment comes out.
But...when things work out the way I expected...
then, I'm on top of my little world...jubilant.
It's really unfortunate...there are anticipations
on most things in life, which causes much stress.
Expectations are truly a state of mind...

What's the solution?

"Acceptance" is the change of attitude called for...
How? Through a wonderful gift called "Choices..."
If I want to continue living my style...
I can...But, if I want more fulfillment in life,
less expectations, I dialogue...I talk of feelings...
Through communication, I learn of others moods,
others ideas, as they learn of mine...if they want to,
and if they don't, my choice is to either accept
or not accept...and live with the consequences.
Easier said than done...but, it can be done...

Today...I Never Really Understood...

When my son Justin was in grade 10, he had to read the book: *To Kill A Mocking Bird* by Harper Lee, for his English class. He had to analyze the story and write up a report. He asked me to proofread his paper. I suggested as a finale that he write a poem. He gave me the ideas that were important to him, and I put them in stanzas. He then corrected my work and made the changes he felt were needed.

A few years later, going through some papers, I came across this poem. Upon re-reading it, I felt a few revisions were needed. But, in the end it was still Justin's poem.

When I think of Justin, I feel his intuitiveness, his sensitivity. Justin has a lot of empathy for the underdog... certainly a good quality. This poem touches home on a lot of bases for him.

Today...I Never Really Understood...

Today...I never really understood...
how, when I was young and innocent, that
I truly believed in things that were not true.
Maycomb had a great influence on my beliefs.
At that time I had an awful prejudice against Boo.

Today...I never really understood...
how Tom could be so wrongfully charged
because of the color of his skin.
It didn't matter who defended him.
Maycomb would never let that person win.

Today...I never really understood...
how people could feel the way they did.
I felt that racism and prejudice were wrong.
Tom and Boo have goodness in their hearts,
just like the mockingbird singing his song.

Today...I never really understood...
until I made the commitment to find out
what it felt like walking in others shoes.
Their pains, their sorrows I truly sensed,
when I considered their points of view.

Today...I never really understood..
how things still remain the same over time.
Why? People have to change from within.
Negative thoughts and actions destroy the soul.
To Kill A Mocking Bird truly is a sin.

Walking the Streets of Individuality

My niece, Elise Hagman, wrote this poem after having read the novel by Harper Lee *To Kill A Mocking Bird*. This was a part of her English Assignment...Here is the results.

I truly enjoyed *To Kill A Mocking Bird*, and after reading Elise's poem, I felt it was very well presented. I'm so pleased to be able to make it a part of this book.

Keep up the good work, Elise. Thank-you for letting me submit your work.

Walking the Streets of Individuality.

The streets of Maycomb were quiet,
Everything so peaceful and calm.
The sun is about to rise,
And the wind, there was none.

The weather is so **Unique**…
It is rarely predictable.
I grab my shoes and my coat,
And just walk around my neighborhood.

The birds sing peacefully as I walk…
While passing Miss Maudie's house I stop.

I picture her out in her coveralls, wearing a straw hat,
Working on her precious azaleas.
"She loved everything that grew in God's earth."
Miss Maudie was **One Of A Kind**.
Not only did she love the earth,
She always found a way to bring the sunshine out.

The bright yellow sun blinds me, so I keep going.
This time I make about two blocks before I stop again.

I was standing in front of Boo Radley's house,
Just thinking of how innocent an isolated person can be.
Being locked up was the way he wanted to live.
That didn't mean he couldn't care about others...about us.
Boo was ORIGINAL and I understood why.

I end the walk in front of my house,
Imagining the distinctive form of...
Atticus Finch, Attorney At Law, Dad!!
A white man who has stuck his neck out for the blacks,
In a time that was dangerous. He risked a lot...we risked a lot.
But Atticus stood up and *Stood Apart.*

We all walk a different path,
But I realize Boo, Miss Maudie, Atticus reflected my image.
We were all walking the street of *Individuality.*

And, May You Find Happiness Today.

I met this gal a while back…there was something about her that drew me towards her. She was so likeable, yet looked like she could use a helping hand from time to time…someone to talk to. She would never ask…Of course not. She was too proud for that.

I don't know what she had heard about me, or perhaps she wasn't interested, but it took me a long time to convince her to put down her defenses and join me for a meal. It turned out very enjoyable for both, and we ended up doing this fairly often. We would talk about everything, and in all honesty, it became a bit of a dilemma for her… wanting to share of herself, yet afraid of letting too many feelings out. She has a lot of fear of really letting her feelings show.

This poem is for you. May you truly enjoy life to it's fullest by risking and trusting of yourself…of your feelings. To do this, enjoy life to it's fullest, enjoy each day as it comes. Whatever concept you have of a God, may he protect and keep you well.

Thanks for being a very special friend.

Note: She has re-married, and seems to be at peace with her choice…therefore at peace with self. She has found her happiness…today…and that's all that counts.

116

And, May You Find Happiness Today.

Happiness: A state of joy and complacency…
A warm feeling of total contentment.

May your wisdom guide your children,
May your love bond you as friends.
May your patience find strength to bend,
yet, may you set limits….both must blend.
May you find kindness when wounds must mend.
May you find courage to make amends.
    And, may you find happiness today.

May your home give warmth and shelter.
May it be cozy during cold winters.
May your designs in crafts only get better.
May you never lose your 'touch' as a baker.
May your walls ring out with laughter…
May these sounds continue to the rafters.
    And, may you find happiness today.

May you forever love your father.
May you perpetually love your mother.
May you always be friends with your sisters.
May you never lose touch with your brothers.
May you provide good roots for your daughters.
May you and your son talk often together.
    And, may you find happiness today.

May your pains and hurts of past years unwind.
May your beautiful eyes maintain their shine.
May you go on searching your wondrous mind.
May you feel comfort in the answers you find.
May you be gentle to yourself...that's fine.
May your heart continue being so kind.
And, may you find happiness today.

May your new love treat you with respect.
May you not lose this bond through neglect.
May you share feelings...not simply deflect.
May you find humility...you're not perfect.
May you realize true love, not merely expect.
May you gamble wisely by stacking the deck.
And, may you find happiness today.

May your concept of God, for you, be clear.
May He grant you health for many years.
May you share with Him your anguish and fears.
May His comfort be sought during the tears.
May He give you strength to look in your mirror.
May you realize that you're very dear.
And, may you find happiness today.

Happiness: A state of joy and complacency...
A warm feeling of total contentment.

The Crossroads of Life.
(A tribute to Julie)

All through life we must make decisions. Decisions concerning job, decisions concerning income, decisions concerning family, and many more personal decisions. It also seems at certain times in life, many decisions are altered or changed completely. Whatever the problem, we must look at the pro's and con's. From there form an opinion. These are the crossroads... what way to go or not to go. Do we take a path already in existence or do we forge our own trail.

My friend Julie...this is where you're at ...decisions... crossroads...where to go, what to do, whom to trust. Julie, take the path you ought...Only you can decide.

My opinion may not be worth a whole lot, but I've come to understand and respect your values, your beliefs. You've always been kind and very honest with me...When need be, you've always told me, in a nice way, if you didn't agree with my thinking... and if you felt that change was appropriate, you'd suggest it.

I enjoyed writing this. Poetry is so beautiful when read and fully understood. Unfortunately this beauty only last a short time...but we can get these feelings back merely by re-reading the poem again. I guess that's life, that's decisions... re-evaluating, feeling good, second guessing, re-evaluating.

This poem is a tribute to you, Julie...Thank-you, my friend.

The Crossroads of Life.
(A Tribute to Julie)

She displays confidence, but is not free.
She hides it well, letting very few see.
Through her disguise, her decisions are based
on much thought. This makes it hard to be traced.
Like the many crossroads of her life,
entwined, needing nourishment to survive.
Her answers, once taken, feed the soul.
A path forms leading her through the fold.
She feels happy, that's the way it should be.
The crossroads of life…A tribute to Julie.

She displays confidence, but is not free,
She hides it well, letting very few see.

"You'll never, ever find
in all the rhymes in a life time,
a way to understand me.
It could never possibly be."
Yet, she turns around and says:
"Hello, little friend of mine. Come in.
The door won't slam in your face.
Let's talk. I don't know where to begin."

Through her disguise, her decisions are based
on much thought. This makes it hard to be traced.

"It's unfortunate I think a lot,
never really saying my thoughts.
Yet, to you I can commit myself.
Many of my feelings come off my shelf."
Such a beautiful woman of class...
I admire her morals, her decisions.
A stylish lady needing no flash
to attract men...She's more than a vision.

Like the many crossroads of her life,
entwined, needing nourishment to survive.

Life compares to a jagged streak of lightning...
At times it becomes very frightening.
At other moments...it's a fascination...
The feelings are very intoxicating.
The crossword puzzle on how to survive
becomes jumbled. Everything is in a faze.
A little food for thought, you continue to strive.
Finally, the solution stares you in the face.

Her answers, once taken, feeds the soul.
A path forms leading her through the fold.

We all have our problems to solve...
Hell, Julie, that's the way life resolves.
Through your truly intelligent mind,
all your answers you will find.
Imagine life without fear...You can you know...
because you're the one who created it.
That's right! Therefore, if you wish to grow,
and I know you do...have faith...use your wit.

She feels happy, that's the way it should be.
The crossroads of life...A tribute to Julie.

Many hours of thought. Some conclusions
have been found to a few of the solutions.
Understanding that things usually workout,
her mask starts to fade, ready for the next bout.
It took me a long time to reach you,
Julie, I hope I don't lose sight of you.
This is a tribute to you, my friend.
I know it's not easy, but time does mend.

The crossroads of life will always exit,
in each and everyone of us till we die.
To get a few answers, we must persist
through a life time...Finally one day
all the answers we will truly find.
That day being in a casket where we lie.

A Deadly Seductive Relationship.

The title really tells it all. I became caught up in a relationship that would probably have harmed me in so many different ways if I had continued on the path I was on.

This relationship was so one sided. Actually, a better description to portray this union would probably be, it was such a lopsided, destructive affair…therefore I'm fortunate that I was finally able to break away from this connection.

It took me years to come to terms with the desire of wanting to start all over again…even though I knew it was such a bad choice, a bad move. Still today, after twenty years of being spilt up, I still hunger for this type of love…yet I'm so very happy that it's over…Contradictions? You bet!

For those of you who've been there, done that…you know exactly what I'm talking about. For those of you who haven't had this 'on the edge' experience, well, all I can say is that you're very, very lucky.

A Deadly Seductive Relationship.

We met when I was quite young…
I was maybe twelve or thirteen.
I remember the first time
I was introduced to you…
I damn near died from fright.
We weren't supposed to be together…
I was so terribly afraid that
my parents would see you with me.

You had a peculiar scent…
something desirable, yet
harsh. I had smelt this
distinctive, educible odor
on other people's attire.
At first, I didn't want to
get too close…just in case
your scent permeated onto me.

I recall the first time we kissed…
Oulala…I just about fainted.
I didn't quite know what to expect,
but, I didn't anticipate that.
I became dizzy, things were turning
around too quickly. I excused
myself and found a place to sit.
I needed to think this through.

In a very short time we became
quite close friends, very chummy…
I had to be careful where we met,
therefore I took my precautions.
We'd meet in some dingy corner
or hidden bushes…never in the open.
You were agreeable and compliant,
always trying so hard to please.

I felt this indescribable joy
every time I was around you.
How you yielded so much power
was beyond me…but I loved it.
Every time I caught a whiff
of your scent, I started to drool.
I became so dependent upon you…
and that's exactly what you wanted.

Oh! You were good at mind games…
and your stakes were high.
I walked into your amusement,
not knowing where I was headed,
and, deep down, not really caring.
Your intentions were to seduce me,
and I wanted you to succeed…
I loved the feeling you brought.

Before too long, our relationship
was known by all, thanks to you.
At first I was quite shy...
You taught me it didn't matter
what people thought or even felt.
It was none of their business,
and if they wished to frown...
that was their problem, not ours.

I remember so vividly caressing
your slim body... breathing deep.
Each night before falling asleep,
you'd surrender to my touches,
letting my lips kiss you to no end.
Often during the night I'd awake,
wanting your taste, your perfume.
Ah! You were such a good lover.

Of course, the mornings were special too.
My eyes weren't even open yet,
and I was groping to find you...
The spans when you went missing,
I'd search frantically everywhere.
The few times you were absent,
thinking I'd lost you, I became edgy...
then you'd appear out of the blue.

This turned out to be a prolonged,
esoteric, intimate correlation.
We both became very obsessive...
You kept getting better and better,
and I kept wanting more and more.
Finally, I had to make some changes...
There was no way I could keep up.
You were wearing me out completely.

But, I didn't want to lose you
psychologically...I just couldn't...
yet, you were killing me, my friend.
One moment I was breaking off...
then, the next I was apologizing,
pleading for your forgiveness.
Finally the time came when...
we both knew it had to end.

A number of years have passed
since we last shared moments...
yet, I still recall vividly
your seductive, addictive power.
I missed you tremendously, my love,
but, today I'm happy it's over.
I've changed a lot...but I see
you haven't changed at all...
my dear charming, deadly Cigarette.

I'm Only a Guest of God's…

I was listening to Elvis sing "Falling in love with you." I love that song, especially the first verse, "Wise men say, only fools rush in…" and I got thinking about all the different expressions, all the different adages I've heard in my lifetime.. WOW! Some are humorous, some quite serious, yet all have a definite message.

Lately, I've kinda gone over the subject of wisdom, truth, honesty in a few different poems…so why again? I guess I'm a slow learner. I need to see things from different angles to finally catch on. Repetition, repetition, repetition… Isn't that how we learn? It is for me.

The verses I've chosen are not better or worse than others. As I got into this poem, they were the one that crept in… therefore I started probing these aphorisms. I was amazed at how many times I have used these sayings in my life…Wow! Hundreds of times…or more.

So where was I going with this poem? As I was writing the verses, I realized that I had experienced all the verses at different times in my life…mostly by encountering, then embedding them into my repertoire. Certainly not all fit my style…in fact most didn't feel real comfortable, therefore I'd let them go, or make adjustments to fit my needs, then I would search for new ones.

Through this search, I also came to realize I was doing some of the things I had been taught…For example…At the end of each day I have to review my day…see if I have done right or wrong, and to rectify, if possible.

How do I go about this? As my Creator's guest, I have the courtesy to ask for His guidance, and thank Him for His direction…and as His guest He gives me freewill to continue making mistakes to ask Him for directions and guidance again. What A Life!!

I'm Only a Guest of God's ...

To be wise doesn't necessarily mean age...
Merely, for one to have experienced the taste...
through blunders...then, having the courage
to admit they are fallible, searching for knowledge
to mend these wrongs...moving on...by turning the page.
Personally, knowing I'm only a guest of God's...
I'm mindful He'll show me the path I must trod.

'Tis a wise man who buys his spouse an arctic mink...
who shows her love and respect and truly listens.
Somebody better clue in the fellow who thinks
he's the boss...Obviously this man is missin'
some of his faculties and needs a shrink...
He'd better get in tune before he starts whistlin'.
You may say: "That is bribery!"...and perhaps so.
A learned man once told me..."Don't be afraid to show
your love you have foresight...by indicating you know
who really is the boss...it saves grief and throes."

Many a wise person has said: "If you worry
about tomorrow, there is no comfort in this day.
Ponder not the future...be not in a hurry.
In all actuality, yesterday's gone...taken away...
and tomorrow, well, it just may never be...
What does that leave you with? One Day...Today...
To make life easier...follow the lamplighter...
pursue his path ...even through miserable weather.
The trail that he's left sure is a lot brighter...
His route leads to places that truly inspire."

Wise people always talk about a journey...
a journey called life...what an experience!
Whatever life-style chosen, nothing's for free...
You have choices: You can choose a life of pretense,
using mind altering substitutes...believing what you see
is true. Make a will, for this style makes no sense...
and probably long before your time you'll be dead!
...Or choose ownership, gaining your daily bread,
by taking on life on life's terms...Go ahead,
try it...but first, your past you must shed...

"Don't forget...What goes around, comes around."
How many times have I heard this comment?...
I'd be afraid to guess! Over the years I've found
this to be true...and difficult to prevent...
especially the demeaning acts...they're bound
to rear up at the most inopportune moments,
often causing me grief. This is called pay back.
Astute people...after many trials...acquire the knack
of looking at issues...not to belittle or detract,
but to see them for what they are, by getting the facts.

I was told more than once: "It's not where
you stand, but where you're going that counts...
a turning point..." The unknown makes me scared.
I'm not sure what I'm looking for...lots of doubt...
By asking God...not my ego...I learn to share...
and listen...The feedback usually helps me out.
It's so neat the feelings felt on a right decision,
even when others think it's wrong...and my vision
they judge. The issues that truly bring elation,
are when I'm right on results affecting my passions.

An old gent told me once, "Opportunity
is a two edged sword." I didn't understand.
"If you want to succeed you must have veracity...
Truth and right circumstances walk hand in hand...
On the other side, if you think you have fecundity
by having no conscience...crushing people like sand...
well, both are opportunities of the same sword...
though of opposite thinking...The side you lean toward
will determine if you wish to share or to hoard.
Who will judge right or wrong?...At day's end...The Lord."

To be wise doesn't necessarily mean age...
Merely, for one to have experienced the taste...
through blunders...then, having the courage
to admit they are fallible, searching for knowledge
to mend these wrongs...moving on...by turning the page.
Personally, knowing I'm only a guest of God's...
I'm mindful He'll show me the path I must trod.

A Young Man's Passions

The following three poems were the writing of a young man meeting the world head on...I was that young man. I wasn't sure if I wanted to add these poems in this book, but in reviewing them, I felt, even though they were written some days ago, they really are timeless.

Here is a collage...an assembly of the three diverse poems. You be the judge...It wouldn't be the first time I'm wrong...nor the last.

It's a Cold Feeling.

In my own thinking, I feel there are many wrongs happening in the world, every second of every day.

Corrupt politics...using fear and tyranny...subjecting their people while robbing them of all their wealth and dignity.

Throughout the whole world there is poverty, but especially in the 3rd world, which leads to death and famine.

Another is spousal abuse...The perpetrator usually takes out their frustrations on the ones they love. In a lot of cases, there is much physical harm, much emotional hurt, especially where children are involved. The scars can and usually do last a life time. And the list goes on...

I get a cold feeling...a very cold feeling.

It's a Cold Feeling.

A shock, when you wake up some morn'
to find your family in mourn...
For that day your mother has gone...
Death is what she finally found.
>It's a cold feeling...
>A very, very cold feeling.

Down and out, and with many debts,
perhaps the ultimate being death,
wondering when it will all end...
Money...you tramp...you bastard friend.
>It's a cold feeling...
>A very, very cold feeling.

Why do people hate and kill?
Why does rage the headline fill?
Why are suicides our main theme,
instead of love? I could just scream!
>It's a cold feeling...
>A very, very cold feeling.

Marriage, we see it every day.
The most popular model portrayed,
is a broken home...and children
suffering...Why don't people try to mend?
>It's a cold feeling...
>A very, very cold feeling.

To gain advantage of someone
is the norm, especially if we
can con him...or we can defeat...
Why must we always cheat?
     It's cold feeling...
     A very, very cold feeling.

To win a war...Is that the price
a man must pay...giving his life
to protect his precious domain?
And, once dead, no Government claims?
     It's a cold feeling...
     A very, very cold feeling.

I'd love to be able to trade
all the above sadness...that's portrayed
as "part of life..." Does it need to be?
Perhaps, if our Creator helped us see
a better path...if we so choose...
living would become more than a ruse...
     for, deception sure is a cold feeling...
     It's a very, very cold feeling.

A Confused Muse...

Have you ever daydreamed? Well this poem is of that nature. Often, I'll sit around and think. Actually, it seems I'm always thinking...and sometimes the thoughts are a bit weird, yet many times they're even well thought out...asking the right questions, for I don't pretend to know it all...in fact I really don't know a whole lot. Often, if I'm in a state of muse, there are so many things I don't understand...I become quite confused.

A Confused Muse...

It sure would be nice someday,
to rehash forgotten memories
with old friends of childhood past...
shelved in the back of my mind.

Since there is only one God...
why don't you pray to your God,
and, I will pray to my God,
in our different places of worship.

Whoever thought up the phrase
"to brown nose"? Quite descriptive,
and so graphic...for those seeking this...
but I'd have to question the taste.

"Thank-you" can be an expression
of honest, sincere gratitude...
"Thank-you" can be an expression
of sincere hurt and rejection...

One summer night, a street named Watt's
erupted into a bloody riot...
And, once upon a Munich Olympic,
there was a gory, deadly massacre...

I wonder how Jewish and Black folk feel?
These two classes of people are blamed
for a lot of the world's problems...
Scapegoats are needed...so, why not these.

One day: "Oh, I love you darling."
Next day: "Oh, I hate you darling."
Is this a board game called opposites?
Before you start...learn the rules...

"Peace" is usually the common word
used by our beautiful young...
"Peeze" is usually the common word
for a foreigner relieving himself...

Navigation of the Mind.

How the mind ceases to wander. In the space of a few seconds, the mind can be in many different situations or thoughts.

We are now boarding the airplane for a trip with my thoughts. The flight has 1) Clearance, 2) Take-off, 3) Navigation, 4) Landing Privileges at each different concept it has created.

I am still trying to define soul. It certainly has to do with the emotional, mental and spiritual feelings I have. I do know, the mind is part of the soul, yet the soul is independent of the mind. It tends to have a different set of rules. It seems to not really care when I'm hurting…but, the end result is… that it does what's right for me.

I'm not sure if you want to come aboard, but if you do…
Welcome aboard. Flight: Number 1

Time: infinite…past, present, future.
Destination: Navigation of the mind.
"All passengers have your boarding passes."

Navigation of the Mind.

The airplane, to destination" Unknown."
…In my mind the big engines roar.
My thoughts are always on a flight,
reaching out to some far distant shore.

Where I choose to land, heaven knows,
I go on any runway that I feel.
Perhaps in a church…to speak to God.
In this mystic setting, in a pew I kneel.

Perchance I pilot amongst some friends
who are of different color and creed.
Each are created accordingly,
having different desires and needs.

Now, my grey cells, they seem to have flown
to strange places, among unwanted foes.
These passengers, I have no need for,
therefore, no desire to want to know.

Then, out of the blue, sadness creeps in…
Broken relations seeking to intrude.
Asking them to leave, by refusing their demands…
I let them know nothing was left to construe.

Wow, the traffic is getting quite heavy...
My sensory system is starting to jam...
I'd better get in touch with my center,
instead of letting everything become crammed.

Things seem to have settled down a bit,
as I look out my window...all is calm...
Now's a good time to steer towards
a warm cozy setting...Why not with palms?

The controller sweeps clear my runway...
My mind is focused...tuned in on love.
It starts on take-off, with my special friend,
and keeps on going far, far above.

The soul is so incomprehensible,
yet beautiful, no matter what it spells.
Through the soul, the navigation of the mind
gives choices...to either keep or dispel...
In other words, try and keep it simple.

My Eyes...The Reflection of My Soul.

Life certainly is a challenge...at least that's the conclusion I've come to...through talking with folks, through listening to what they have to say...and I am a good listener, through experiences...through observation.

Break-up of a relationship, be it spouse...married/common law, be it friendship, be it children and their rebellious ways...whatever...It Hurts. Think about it...we have different levels of hurt, even though each affects us intimately...and these levels change as we change. For example, as we grow older our priorities change, our values change, our beliefs my even change.

This poem stems from this thought process...break-up, hurts, change. Sounds simple, but it's not. The death of a relationship causes the most stress. It affects nearly every emotion a person has experienced, it causes so much damage...sometimes physical, always mental/emotional... thoughts/feelings, more often than not, spiritual, and if there are children, well I won't even go there.

How do I observe? Through my eyes...which see all...the good, the bad, the indifferent. In understanding my soul, knowing that it is of me, yet very much it's own boss...guiding me in what is truly right, not necessarily what I think is right, then what my eyes observe...this mirror image to my soul...this reflection, eventually will stimulate the soul into the right changes. I may not like them...and the soul cares less...they will still be the right changes.

Again, it is others who have given me the ideas for this poem...Thank-you! Meaningful conversation always has stimulated my imagination...and I hope will continue to do so.

My Eyes...The Reflection of My Soul.

I'm so, so tired...
I need to rest, to relax...but I can't.
I won't let fear take control of my emotions,
not a chance...I won't give-in, I shan't.
I know I'm swirling in my mind's ocean...
wondering how I helped create this problem,
let alone how to go about solving this gem...
I know not the answer to this mayhem.

Because of past issues being presented today,
I feel a lot of anxiety when you're near...
Why? Your voice is so harsh, much cacophony.
Knowing how kind you were...that brings a tear.
Religion talks of heaven and hell...right or wrong...
I choose the former, even though I've strayed,
and just thinking of the later, I don't belong...
Hell is a stopping place when folks are afraid.

I need time for me...
But then all I do is rehash memories...
and that's not good...I solve nothing.
Friends have suggested to get on my knees...
a bit of humility that certainly brings.
Another proposal...pen, paper, solitude, and write...
Only I know my intuitions, my plight,
therefore, get on board...discover the flight.

Searching deep into my soul...my feelings
for answers, I ask myself "what's the questions?"
Is it all his fault? Who's doing the dealing?"
To understand all the causes of this contention,
I need to be honest in my search for solutions...
I must comprehend to differentiate between
surface and underlying answers...no more collusions...
I'm just so tired of all his plots and schemes..

My eyelids are so heavy...
I think I'm going to try and calm the images
my mind has created...by closing my eyes...
I wonder if I could sort all the different pages,
the emotional and the mental ones...then categories.
All I ever wanted was to be respected and loved.
All you ever wanted was control. I felt engulfed...
overpowered. Summoning my courage, I'd had enough.

I often wonder why some of my dreams
remind me of a strong wind? I guess because
of the debris left behind...thoughts that seems
to be fragmented, yet, are part of the cause.
Dealing with unfinished business is not fun...
Lots of the issues I have no control...
plus, we're on different wave lengths...no one
wins, in fact we're both losers in this poll.

I will to keep my eyes open…
but I can't. Different pictures crowd
my ethos, all demanding immediate attention.
Wow! Some of those photos, I'm not too proud…
I must have been protecting myself with pretensions.
Looking at it with some honesty…several charades
distinguish themselves with clarity…I'm afraid…
but, truthfully…I'm not too scared to wade.

I've come to realize, life includes many factors
I have no rule over…therefore, I can't give-up
on my beliefs. I've become tired of us being actors,
seeking to play many roles. In no time, my cup
was spilling. You wanted no part of this mess,
placing all the fault on me…then, 'Mr. Clean'
offers himself as my savior…trying to caress
my mind, body and soul. Jerk! In your dreams.

If I could only sleep…
My whole being needs repose…I'm beat.
I wish you could see life through my eyes,
how I really try and keep things neat,
that I don't need to live shrouded in disguises…
But you can't…yet, by your actions, you convey
that you believe you can continue to stray
and enter my mind at will…all without my say.

Tasting your antics, I really need to escape
from you, by taking an emotional break...
eluding your features, giving me a chance to gape,
to gaze at why you want my soul to ache.
Some of these images just don't make sense...
You're afraid to look inside...to truly admit
fault. You blame me, then put up defenses
to feed your ego...That takes a lot of wit.

That sleep felt so good...
Yesterday is a faded mist...where you belong.
I loved what you were, not what you've become,
therefore I want nothing from you...So long...
I really hope the best for you, not merely crumbs.
From back when...to today, we've paid a heavy toll.
Please, let's make it end...that's my goal.
The pain in my eyes is a reflection of my soul.

To find fault is easy, to change is not.
I want joy, not sadness, and the answer is time.
There are issues my Higher Power has taught...
one being forgiveness...this healing power is mine
if I want it...and I do. Perhaps you won't embrace.
My biggest asset is my past...not to live, but use
as a guide...to learn from mistakes and praise
my good deeds. Please, let me experience my muses.

You Give Your Voice So Sweetly.

While living in Saskatoon, a friend told me about these two sisters living in the north end of the city...in fact I went with him to a party at their home. I had a great time, at least that's what they tell me...and I'm sure I did.

After that week-end, I got to know these gals fairly well. One of the sisters, Judy, is a superb musician. This poem is written for her.

She has a charming personality, gracious looks, and a super voice. While strumming her guitar or playing the piano, her voice reminds me, metaphorically, of an angel.

I prefer her guitar playing, while she prefers the piano. Immaterial, she's excellent with both instruments...plus she gives her voice so sweetly. I hope, over time, the only changes you make musically are not really changes, but challenges.

Note:

Over the years I have lost contact with Judy. The last verse I wrote just recently...It would be a real blast to get together with her. Of course, she'd have to sing for me.

You Give Your Voice So Sweetly.

Remember when we met a while back?
I do. Wow! we sure did have some fun times.
Being me...my disposition didn't lack...
You sat back and laughed. You thought it was fine.

I came often to your quaint little suite.
I enjoyed the ambiance to no extent.
A great big smile was your way to greet...
especially when I was in the mood to vent.
      You give your voice so sweetly.

I laughed often of your portrait...
but beautiful you certainly are.
To the lucky man who will be your mate,
you'll make him feel like a brilliant star.

The first time I heard you play your guitar,
I sat back...curious of what was to come.
Then, this capricious voice from afar
expounded. My body tingled...I felt numb...
      You give your voice so sweetly.

At every occasion I'd ask you to sing...
I loved it. The impressions that I felt
were of infinite joy. You're truly something...
the feelings you'd awaken...then you'd quell.
      You give your voice so sweetly.

I'm quite positive God was not bemused
when he gave you your abilities.
Perhaps he mused, then became amused
with the wonder that he made, with such ease.

Music is your soul…singing your passion…
and because of it you are the winner…
A natural talent with much fashion,
sharing your gifts without surrender.
     You give you voice so sweetly.

As the years roll away, I'll wonder of
you, where you landed…for this won't last…
I'm a wanderer…one day I'll saunter off…
losing contact. Soon, it'll be merely past.
     Whatever the turn please, always be you…
     Keep on singing, keep on smiling.
     I was the fortunate one. You construed,
     through your music, oh so many things.
     Always giving of your voice so sweetly.

The years have come…where have they gone?
I know not what became of you, my friend,
yet, sometimes, I imagine you singing a song.
I close my eyes, sit back and pretend…
     Wherever you are, may your voice extol
     in song, expressing love and happiness,
     especially for those closest to your soul…
     your partner and children…nothing less.
     You gave your voice so sweetly.

God willing, one day we will meet again…I can't wait!

Don't Ever Say Goodbye.

This is one of those poems where I can honestly say," Where did you come from?" I had no intentions of writing any poem…I was merely tidying up a few, changing a word or line, and in some I added new stanzas. I do this every once in a while…a fine-tuning.

Trying to change the character of one of my poems, I wrote the first line, "I couldn't have missed her…there was just no way"…my mind started visioning all these different scenarios. I figured, "Why not!" and away I went. Everything fell into place…the title, the verse, the different schemes in rhyming …everything.

Thinking back, I remember a scene similar to this in Saskatoon. I was sitting in some lounge, and this good looking gal was already singing by the time I had entered. I recall her talking about this guy who had played in that particular band, and it seems had died. They were singing and playing his music in tribute. I don't know what he died from, nor his name, and the gal never talked to me…plus his music wasn't really my type.

A musician friend committed suicide a number of years ago…Was that part of the reason for writing this? I don't know. Finally, I told myself, leave it be. It's a poem with a good, yet sad story. Actually there are two poems in this poem…and that was interesting!

Storytelling through poetry is a real challenge, yet the feelings when finished are just as rewarding. You make the call.

Don't Ever Say Goodbye.

I couldn't have missed her…there was just no way…
What a beauty…A real stunner, actually.
Trying real hard not to be noticed, all eyes
were on her. Sitting down, she ordered coke and rye.
Checking out the scene, a couple of the guys
ask if they can join her. Nodding, she complies.
Trying to impress, the jockeying starts right away…
for, these guys are merely glands wanting this stray.

Experiencing the moment, a slight smile
appears, 'cause for her it's been a while.
Someone at her table tells a crude joke…
Asking him to refrain, another offers a toke.
Saying no, she asks them what kind of folk
they thought she was? Perhaps a tramp, or on dope,
or someone they could easily take advantage of?
Getting up, she excused herself…she'd had enough!

Walking to the bar, she sits in the stool next to me.
Having observed her actions, I pretend I don't see
her coming. Turning, I greet her with a warm grin.
Glancing at her fingers, I noticed a wedding ring…
C'est la vie! Some I lose, though sometimes I do win.
In the mirrors reflection, I sense a state of chagrin…
Introducing myself, I ask if she'd like a drink.
Clinking glasses in acknowledgment, I give her a wink.

"Do you come here often," she asks. "Yah! Often as I can."
"A while back, this is where I met my husband…
it sure brings back mem'ries. We met one September…
it takes a long time to cool passionate embers."
Looking around the bar, she notices the band members.
A big smile appears…friends that she remembers.
Each comes over, whisper something, give her a big hug.
Sadly wiping away the tears, she merely shrugs.

Feeling very awkward, not knowing what to say,
I say nothing. Noticing her turn her ring in play
she says to me, "My guy use to play with this band…
actually, we both did. I sang…he played bass, and
wrote. I loved his ballads. He sure had the hand.
When I found that last love song he wrote, I ran."
"What happened to him?" I ask. "He died of cancer…
wasted away. I'm still searching for answers."

"I heard the guys were playing a tribute here tonight.
I wanted to come, but didn't…I came in spite…"
The band started to play. Listening, some tears appear.
"That was a favorite of his: 'Love has no fear.'
Wow!! Do I miss him? I feel his presence…so near."
"I've got to leave…the ghosts are starting to peer."
Getting up to go, someone from the stage called to her.
After a moment's hesitation, she goes over and confers.

Getting up on the platform, to the microphone she walks.
"Good evening to all. I was asked to come and unlock
the vault to my heart...Only one man had that key..."
"How many of you remember my partner Lanky Lennie?
Wow! A lot of you do. It looks like we must agree...
HE WAS GREAT! Billy has asked me to sing...let me see...
Phew! I wasn't expecting this..." Turning to the drummer,
she nods. "Here's one called, 'Life's a real bummer.'"

"She's a doll," I state to myself, "and she can sing!"
Looking around, I notice everyone's truly listening.
Her voice and body language certainly concurred...
the love she expressed told me how she suffered.
She cast her feelings through Lennie's songs...in offer...
Her melodies, her harmonies, blended so well together.
Standing so very fragile, the tears telling no lie.
"Here's Lenny's last song, 'Don't ever say goodbye.'"

"Before I start, I'm not sure if I'll be able
to finish this song. Understand, if I'm unable,
it's in knowing, for me to sing it is too painful."
"This was his final song, written from his soul.
He wrote it to me, for me, and it is so beautiful...
I love and miss him so much. I've felt the toll."
Standing center stage, acoustic guitar in hand,
she sang of his feelings for her, his woman.

"You'll never know how much I love you, girl.
You'll never know how much I really care...
Looking into your eyes, all I see are pearls...
beautiful gems embedded in an angelic visage.
You've always been good to me, letting me share
your soul, letting me taste your wondrous courage."

Tears in my eyes, I hear the piano blending
its sound to her tune...the key man lending
another dimension to the song. From his corner,
the bass guitarist merges in...He's no foreigner
to jammin'. I become aware of the lead's sound,
and the drums' echoing softness...total surround!

"I can remember nearly every time I lied
to you...you always forgave me with a smile.
I also recall all the times you cried
because of my tongue. Often I made you blue...
What a jerk...I was in complete denial...
thinking I needed no one, not even you."

"I've always been afraid to ask the why's...
Why you chose me, not accepting any alibi?
I love you so much. Without you, I'd want to die.
You became my partner...lover, friend, and ally.
My fate...I give to you. I promise to comply.
Don't ever leave me...don't ever say goodbye."

The bar is in total silence. Everyone's listening,
each empathizing with her feelings about missing…
missing his joy, missing his love and affection,
missing his physical being…his impulsive attraction.
She looks so lost, so frail…total consumption
of her grief for this man. She's left no assumptions.

"I will never forget our wedding day…Never!
You were gorgeous. I was one lucky dude…
The love you gave, should last me forever,
yet, I felt so much pain. I damn near did it…
Thank God you understood…most misconstrued.
You found the courage to help me…not to quit."

"Each morning, upon awakening, your fragrant,
aromatic scent is a reminder of how fortunate
I am. I know that while I'm with you, I can't
take your love for granted…that would be a sin…
Rolling over, I hug and cuddle you, enjoying that
moment of lucidity before our day begins."

Finding a Kleenex to drab my eyes, I sense
her eyes on me. Her look is asking: "What, by chance
are you crying about? Are you feeling unhappy?"
I raise my glass in a toast, nodding slightly,
I give her a gentle crease, passing for a smile.
Looking away, she sings of Lennie's intimate style.

"One day, not so long ago, I realized
that I love you, girl, more than I love myself.
It is possible through my dreams…how I contrive
our relationship…for you've always given,
while I've always taken, depleting the wealth.
Today, loving you to the fullest is my mission."

"I've always been afraid to ask the why's…
Why you chose me, not accepting any alibi?
I love you so much. Without you, I'd want to die.
You became my partner…lover, friend, and ally.
My fate…to give to you. I promise to comply.
Don't ever leave me…don't ever say goodbye."

Raising her hand, the band prepares to stop…
watching them attentively, her hand suddenly dropped.
The silence, shattered by a thunderous ovation,
shook the bar. Calling to her in subdued jubilation,
she strummed a few chords on her guitar and said:
"I wrote two verse to you, Lennie…it's in my head.
I'll sing it this once, out of respect…I feel bound."
The hush in the crowd was total: Nary a sound.

"Watching you suffer, not knowing the pain you felt,
that broke my heart, so I tried to be strong…
to take some of your hurt. Both of us were dealt
a bad hand, and both of us died…You the physical,
my best friend and lover. My one true love…gone…
I succumbed to the pain. My death was emotional."

"You asked me to never say goodbye…well my love,
I have to say goodbye, so I may start living.
Your presence is always near, similar to a glove…
like feeling you on my skin. You can be certain,
I'll never forget you…and, yes, you're forgiven.
This is our final act together…no more hurtin'…
This is my closure…I have dropped the curtain."

By acknowledging the crowd, she'd turned the page.
She thanked the band and walked off the stage.
Walking to the bar, for she had forgotten her keys,
she said: "I really respected your allowing me to see,
through your empathy, my feelings towards Lennie…
Thanks. By saying goodbye, I feel a bit free."
I got up and hugged her. Turning, she walked away.
In the far corner I could hear the jute box play…

Concerning the Heart, Logic Need Not Apply.

This poem is written to Deene, to thank her for what she was and for what she meant to me in all the lovely months we were together.

We did break-up, thanks to my strong feelings of no commitments, yet my feelings for her are still very precious, and I hope she continues to smile that radiant smile and not change her beautiful ways.

My nick-name for her was "Sweety-Bum." For what it's worth, it was a different way to express my feelings of endearment towards her.

Concerning the Heart, Logic Need Not Apply.

Love: The famous four letter word,
which, can extract such acute meanings.
A thing of beauty causing so much pain…
going straight for the heart, the feelings…
Then…in the next heart beat…what I gain
if I forgive, is an emotional healing.
In not understanding love, often I hoard.

We met such a long time ago,
yet, it seems like only yesterday.
My! how time just goes and goes,
leaving merely sketches behind.
Looking around…I couldn't stay…
because if I did I wouldn't be kind.

I felt uncomfortable…desiring
no commitments, no responsibilities.
For me, the charades were quite tiring…
You were fully into the heart stuff…
I was too smart for that…this was so silly,
and, what did this have to do with love?

I couldn't see what you saw in a jerk
like me. You really tried to compromise...
I disliked me...my mirror...how could it work?
It couldn't...and I aimed for that goal...
A lot of my truths were simply lies...
and I conveyed this by teasing...to cajole.

Your love was way stronger than mine,
therefore we broke-up...as friends should.
Fancy restaurant, we wined and dined.
We danced, we talked, we laughed, we cried.
A night to remember...it was good,
but, before we said our good-byes...
    you asked:"Why can't you love me?"
    as the tears descended slowly.
    Only I didn't want you to see
    my grief, so I kissed you tenderly.
    At the station, I shared my pain...
    One last kiss...you boarded your train.

Through the windows reflecting skies,
long golden hair and grey/green eyes.
Your appearance mirrored your love,
in contrast to my blues I disguised.
Soft and gentle, like a dove.
Your leaving left me a lot wiser...
    And, what lessons was I taught?
    Love is freely given, not bought.
    While I mostly took, you brought...
    joy and contentment...that's a lot.
    By pardoning my foolishness,
    you also taught me forgiveness.
    In retrospect I learnt...my oh my!
    Through my head games our bond died...
    Your heart wanted no logic to apply...
    and, yes, I do love you!

And in the whispers I hear her say:
"Do you love me?" "Do you love me?"

Love Is Not a One Time Gift.

I had a dream not so long ago, and you, Aunt Lucille, were a part of that dream. I was surprised that I remembered this particular dream, for I rarely recall the majority of my dreams. I got thinking about it the next day, and I feel the reason I remembered it was that it had taken place around Dad's anniversary. I truly do miss Dad a lot.

The next day I thought about this dream...those few minutes...It made me want to write a poem. Contemplating a title...it just came to me. I started writing, not quite sure where this would lead. Here is the result.

Thank-you on my behalf, and I think I can say it for the rest of the family, also. The love you give us is very special...truly a gift. I love you very much.

Love Is Not a One Time Gift.

As I walk through life, I experience
the choices I made on the roads I chose.
A time will come when I will be judged
on these selections. How will I be arbitrated?
On my standards of life…truths I debated…
not the goods that caused that arduous trudge.
I will be assessed on morals and values,
not status, which is merely a pretense.

A very good teacher with much sensitivity…
your feature, your trademark is acuity.
Wise in the choice of words, you aren't afraid
to instill what is truth, without the accolades,
plus, much is avowed because you elucidate,
you clarify your position. You don't prevaricate
or deviate from veracity. A very tough act
for others to follow, for you rarely look back.

I remember many years ago, you stated that I should
course my own path, learn from the bad and the good,
and because of it I would be the victor, the winner.
Now I realize that you knew I would not concur…
that I felt I was too smart to learn from elders,
and away I went. The irony is, today I would conjure
for young folk to at least look at the path offered,
but, it won't happen. Therefore, have fun and suffer.

As I traipse through my mind, the word wealth
appears. I start thinking: Yah, it would be nice
materially to be affluent, but there sure is more,
a lot more to be taken into consideration…
like feelings of personal growth and good health,
also, the right intents…but, will that suffice?
No! The amount I give of self, and feel no rancor,
are the measures used to abide my intentions.

What a revelation when fear knocks on the door
and love answers. The trepidation is no more,
gone, and a feeling of warmth rushes through my soul,
yet, I feel doubt…My mind knows how to cajole,
how to twist my feelings. This has taken its toll.
One view taught by you is to appreciate the whole,
not merely its sum parts. Not to always react,
but learn to respond by using a bit of tack.

Love's paradox…the ones we love eminently
are the ones we hurt the most, doesn't come into play
where you're concerned. Your love is your word…
and, thank God it's not something you hoard.
Sometimes, you're not afraid to shake up my comfort
by questioning my actions, if you're not in accord…
By holding back, you're not giving of your feelings,
and invariably, for me, there won't be any healing.

Why is it most of us are looking for greatness
when, really, that doesn't mean a whole lot?
Actually, in the scheme of things, goodness
is the key word…what we do for our friends,
our loved ones, and if need be, to try and mend
the fabric we have damaged. At times, to redress
a situation, a bit of humility is what we sought,
remembering we probably were the cause of the mess.

In life, I certainly carry a lot of extra baggage…
trivia I have no use for, so to the mind's storage
I consign them. But why? The answer is…let them go.
Like a computer, use delete…put an end to that show.
A real freedom will occur…now fresh ideas may grow.
Some of the thoughts I should cultivate and hoe
are memories and dreams…the attained and attainable.
Both you've done. I need to follow you're example.

To say that love is a gift and is recurrent
or recyclable, certainly is true and concurrent.
I can give it over and over again without fear.
In some instances I've used you as my mirror
in which to gauge. You have always been very clear
in your intent, yet at times you've shed some tears
with and for me. Your love you didn't confine
I am so lucky! You are a beautiful paradigm!

I am so fortunate to have you...Your wisdom,
your prudence and good judgment are just some
of the many attributes I can choose from.
My love to you as your love to me
is not a one-time gift, and it's free!
You are one of the very few who has a key
to my heart. Handle with care...please.

Mein Vater.

Where did it all start for me? Of course, my parents. Mom had a very strong influence when I was a child. Family say I am much like her. She died so very young...I sure miss her a lot.

Claire, also, had a big influence, but by the time I really got to know her, I was starting my own life. Now, Dad...his presence...because of the strong character he presented...had the biggest influence on how I should conduct my life.

Dad has done well for himself. It is something I admire and I hope to attain in my lifetime. He has many morals, which he tried to instill in me. He seems to walk the walk, but I have to learn to walk my own walk... by evaluating some of his morals, trying them out...seeing if they fit. To be honest, many I won't change.

I love you, Dad. Living in Hamburg has been a good experience, plus, I've come to realize the security and love you projected. Some time ago you stated, after my accident, 'He's never been the same since.' You maybe right...maybe I'm growing up...following my own lead instead of yours...things you taught me. Thanks!

Je t'aime.

Gerry.

Mein Vater.

Tradition: The folklore, the legends...
all part of my heritage...passed down
through the ages. As his father did...
Dad will pass it on to me...to maintain,
until I pass it on to my sons.

A little Frenchman with piercing
coal like eyes, yet a big heart.
A man who's not afraid to stand-up
for what he believes in, his rights.
    Das ist mein Vater.

Dad's very loud...you can hear him
a mile away...and very explicit...
yet, when he gets serious, my friend,
he doesn't raise his voice. Watch out....
    Das ist mein Vater.

Each of us has had some hardships...
Some more so than others. Looking back,
he seems to have attained more happiness...
by choice...for there is much he desires.
    Das ist mein Vater.

A different character, come what may.
Optimistic, yet so very superstitious...
He believes in God, yet fears black cats,
Friday the 13th, and going under ladders...
    Das ist mein Vater.

By some standards, he is very rich…
Some money…but more so personal wealth.
Striving to make a good, clean living,
I know he desires that I do the same.
Das ist mein Vater.

He's been very fortunate, women wise.
Him and mom weren't always in harmony,
yet, there was much respect…much love.
Mom died so young…Dad truly grieved.
He couldn't live alone…that wasn't life.
Someone was surely taking care of him,
by interposing Claire as part of our family.
Her love encourages Dad to truly be himself.
Das ist mein Vater.

He knows a lot of different people…
of varied ilk…yet claims few friends.
His benchmarks are very high…few achieve…
yet, goes out of his way to help the trodden.
Das ist mein Vater.

I can't speak for my siblings…
they've learnt from Dad how to do that…
but, I do know he's affected each of us.
Not all his examples I'll take…but a lot.
Das ist mein Vater.

Dad has a strong spiritual conviction…
a firm belief in a Higher Power…
and, believes each must find their own.
Nice thing…He's not afraid to show his.
     Das ist mein Vater.

Dad has gained much inner strength
through his twelve step program.
He's come to terms with lots of issues,
and, has made his amends for most of them.
In my eyes that takes a real man.
     Das ist mein Vater.

I love you so very much, Dad,
even though, at times, I don't show it.
Your footprints, I will not walk in…
but, I hope someday to walk beside them,
if I continue the tradition you passed on.
     Das ist mein Vater.

          Tradition: The folklore, the legends…
          all part of my heritage…passed down
          through the ages. As his father did…
          Dad will pass it on to me…to maintain,
          until I pass it on to my sons.

Wherever You Go, I'll Be with You

When I was living in Hamburg, Germany, many years ago, I spent one Christmas alone. What a desolate feeling. To help my loneliness I sat in a bar all night and got totally pissed.

Prior to that evening, I had written a poem called "The One Day Child." This poem is about kids put into Group Homes, for many reasons, mostly broken homes. I used as example one young fellow I got to know a little bit, who eventually ended up in one of these homes. He really was a nice kid, caught up in the turmoil of his parents. He ended up being the loser. The story I use in the poem is not his story...only my imagination.

So, here I am sitting in this bar, feeling so sorry for myself. In my mind I was toasting everybody. Eventually I toasted "Zeke." I recall wondering how he was that night, what he'd gotten for gifts, if his parents had even come to see him or take him out for a night...and that made me sadder.

That's where this story stems from. I imagined all types of scenarios for this little gaffer. Over the years I've always wanted to put together a story where Zeke would be the winner.

I'm not sure why the story unfolded as it did, but the "Spirit of Christmas" seemed like the 'right' type of story, plus the challenge of writing it in rhyme.

Many miracles have happened at Christmas...many people have been given a chance...a chance to forgive, a chance to love again, a chance to express a true joy, a chance to feel a peace within oneself, and to extend it to others...all miracles.

This is my miracle from my thoughts...always with the hope that maybe Zeke did get the opportunity to have been an inspiration...a miracle for someone. It's certainly possible.

I have no clue whatever happened to him...Today I don't think of him too often, but he does pop up in my mind from time to time...so I guess he's still with me wherever I go. Thank-you Zeke for this poem. I wish I had this chalet mentioned in the poem...Ah well, it's nice to dream...Perhaps a miracle?

Wherever You Go, I'll Be with You.

"Hey you jerk! Watch where you're going.
Keep that up...We'll both need a towing."
Some people can't drive...I get so mad.
I can't wait to get back to my pad,
make a hot toddy...just like that TV ad.
Man! Every year it's always the same crap.
I always seem to fall into in their trap...
invariably. Christmas is not fun at all...
I'm at the point where I hate malls.

Businesses during this time should be ashamed...
making people feel they must play their game.
They entice folks with attractive displays...
plus, they give you thirteen months grace to pay!
Consumerism! Yuck! Give me back the old ways...
I loved the sleigh...pulled by a team of horses,
hearing the bells jingling, following the course
of the driver...caroling loudly, sitting on straw...
accepting the cold, knowing my feet will thaw.

I think this Christmas I'm going to my cabin,
setup a small pine, as a symbol, then begin
to enjoy repose and serenity ...in solitude.
I already feel the warmth of the crackling wood...
a pungent yet sweet odor...creating a mood
of inner peace...as I sit near the fireplace,
relaxing, enjoying time out from life's race.
If, by chance, a few friends do come out...
great...touch back a few, without a doubt.

I finally made it! I love it out here…
Oh! Nibbling on some bark is a couple of deer.
Noticing me watching, they slowly walk away.
Hauling in my food and gear, I plan to stay
a few days. Out my window I see a blue jay,
perched on his pulpit, preaching to the world…
then maybe not. It looks like it's the squirrel
he's squawking at, asking him to leave food.
The rodent cares not…His worry is his brood.

Christmas Eve; Big fluffy flakes coming down…
in silence…leaving wetness without a sound.
Walking into this snowy blanket, a peace
enters my realm…I'm lucky! My life's' lease
is intact, and today, by choice, I cease
to be drawn into the passions and emotions
of living…No, this night is a celebration…
What's that sound? Someone is behind my shed.
To not frighten them, cautiously I tread.

"Hey! What are you doing hiding back there?
Come on out. You don't need to be scared."
"Are you hiding from the law? You're quite young…
What's the matter? Has the cat got your tongue?
Please! I want to help. Tell me what you've done."
Walking out with his dog, a slight tremble
I do notice. He looks so meek, so very humble.
"I don't mean to bo..bother you and be so bo..bold…
We haven't eaten in two days…I'm really co..cold…"

"My name's Zeke, and this is my dog Charlie.
Wa…water would be nice…I'm really thirsty.
I gotta get my th..thinking straight…My head hurts…"
Portraying a woeful smile, I felt him conjure,
appealing to my offer for a bit of comfort.
Inviting him into the cozy warmth of my cabin,
I asked where he called home, and about his kin.
"What I'd really like is a bo..bowl of soup,
and a pl..place to rest my head…then the scoop."

'So this is Christmas…' "I love Lennon's song…
If m…man lived those words, what could go wrong?"
Zeke had awoken. Glancing about the room,
he found my chair. He notices the sun's day soon
will be over. Sitting, still humming that tune,
Charlie sat beside him. "Why are you here?" I asked.
Thinking it over, he said: "I wear n..no mask."
Not understanding, I asked him what he meant.
Looking at the dimming fire, he states he was sent.

"I don't understand!" "Neither do I" he said.
"When someone isn't well spiritually, I'm led
to them. Is that your ca..case? Here's my story."
"I think you can tell I'm not seeking glory,
but, if you feel I am, there's no need to wo..worry,
I'm not. I'm a ha..handicapped man…some call
me special…I like that. I have a drawl
when I speak, because of an im..impediment.
Sorry about the me..mess…It wasn't me..meant."

Zeke talked late into the night…none stop.
His story left me in awe. His dad was a cop…
a demanding man. He hated his son's handicaps.
To make up for his failure, he used the strap,
often. Finally, Zeke had had enough of that crap.
He ran away…but he ended up in a bad crowd.
He stole, did drugs…everything was allowed…
He became disillusioned…so tired of the taking.
Ready to throw in the towel, he felt an awakening.

This man was a gift sent by some power…
He spoke of love, of joy…to him and others…
The peace I felt listening to his words,
I can't describe. All the phrases I'd heard
before, yet, my emotions he really stirred
by his comments. He talked about peace…
a freedom he always felt, that never ceased.
"When you're in tune with your thoughts,
they'll harmonize with the emotions you brought."

Upon awakening Christmas morn, on my night table
lay a charm of baby Jesus in the stable.
Puzzled, I notice a note beside the amulet.
It read: "Wear this medallion on a bracelet…
to remind you that your only sure bet
in life is this babe, lying in a manger.
When things are tough, He's the greatest wager
you can place. Apply peace, joy, love…the tools
I left with you. These are very precious jewels…"

Flipping the torn page, I was completely astounded.
I couldn't believe the fortune that I'd found…
"…to be utilized properly…and I know you will.
When in doubt, don't be afraid to stand still…
and listen to your heart…you're spirit is ill,
but easily mended. Just ask…The answers you feel,
will salve your soul. God is love…He will heal."
"Sorry about the mess, I write like a geek…
Merry Christmas. I'll be keeping tabs…Zeke."

Under the squiggly lines of something he drew,
P.S. "Wherever you may go, I'll be with you."
Folding the note, I felt a calmness in me,
realizing he'd given me 'How to live,' for free…
What was it he had said…"Don't just feel…Be…"
"Thank-you whoever you are," I repeated, to-self
This person had given me so much gratis wealth…
on Jesus's birthday…I'm not sure why I was chosen
for this gift…but I do. I have fences to mend.

Many thanks Jesus for sending Zeke…first of all,
for I sense that You sent him on this prowl.
Secondly, Happy Birthday…my best one ever.
Zeke talked of two words…'inspire' and 'endeavor…'
to 'be in spirit,' and 'to strive for whatever'…
I love 'The Spirit of Christmas'…its representation,
Peace and Goodwill, mingled with caresses of affection…
Wherever I go, please tag along…for fun.
That way I'll be in spirit to strive…not run.

It's Neither Here Nor There...
(but it is)...

In all the poems presented...
I had to have lived...or visualized the emotions
expressed...then transcribe what it meant to me...
how it had affected me, how it helped me to focus,
pushing me to analyze, to examine my bias...
see if the new thoughts, the new ideas were valid,
by inspecting the influences...people, place, things,
and make the necessary changes to better me...
Many times I've made mistakes...I'm sure I'll continue,
yet, these new impacts have had noticeable results,
helping me understand that my life really matters...
through family, friends, and my Higher Power...

But, when it comes right down to it...
who cares if I'm a writer? I'm not that important.
Me, of course, and, I suppose, a few friends...
people I may have touched by my words, by my actions,
knowing they've gained to their advantage as I have.
Maybe my family...I realize for most people
it doesn't really matter one way or the other...
It's neither here nor there...Yet, if they're willing
to examine my thoughts, they then have the right
to say yea or nay. Communication is so essential,
as is listening, as is actions...Do you know what?
I matter, you matter...and that's all that really matters...

Glossary

Mme Aucourant:	Mrs. Know it all.
Allô:	Hello.
Non:	No.
Hector Perdant:	Family name/Hector "The Loser."
Dr. Bonhumeur:	Dr. Humourous.
Laflamme:	Family name/The Flame.
Ça Va?:	How are you?
Curé Le Pécheur:	Father the fisherman/ Father the sinner.
Le vieux Bazzou:	The old Jalopy.
Les Désaccord:	The "Out of tune"/ Band name.
Ti-Cul le frappé:	Little smart aleck.
Le gros:	The big or Big.
Merci Seigneur:	Thank God.
L'épouvantail:	Scarecrow.
Ti-Pit:	Nickname "Tiny."
Tourtière:	French Canadian meat pie.
Maudit:	Damn/darn.
Chère:	Dear.
Une Neuvaine:	A Novena.
Vielle:	Old Woman.
Ca m' pue au nez:	Leaves a foul odor/smell.
Yeux Croche:	Cross-eyed.

Printed in the United States
44353LVS00002B/226-456